BLUE & WHITE
EMBROIDERY

Elegant Projects Using Classic Motifs and Colors

KOZUE YAZAWA

TUTTLE Publishing

Tokyo | Rutland, Vermont | Singapore

CONTENTS

 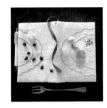   

The color of the ocean
is a blend of iron blue
and gray.

The hue of delicious meringue
is a blend of milky white and
snow white.

The historic buildings
of Yokohama are a blend
of aquamarine and khaki.

IN SEARCH OF COLORS

The seaside where I collect shells.

Yokohama walks in casual clothes.

That certain forest hike.

In a quiet room with the cats, watching the rise and fall

of their rounded stomachs as they breathe in sleep.

Felt with my eyes and ears and skin, gathered in my mind

and heart—all the places, the colors and shapes,

the light and the scents.

As I combine and blend the embroidery threads, I gather the

colors and shapes from the drifting forms in my head.

Blue and white, and the evocative moments glimpsed

between the two colors;

How happy I am to share this beauty with you.

Kozue Yazawa

THE PROJECTS

BOATING
MOTIF

Cloth with Appliquéd Anchor ● instructions on page 66

A COAT OF ARMS FOR
A SEAFARING COUNTRY

Hand Towel Embroidery   instructions on page 66

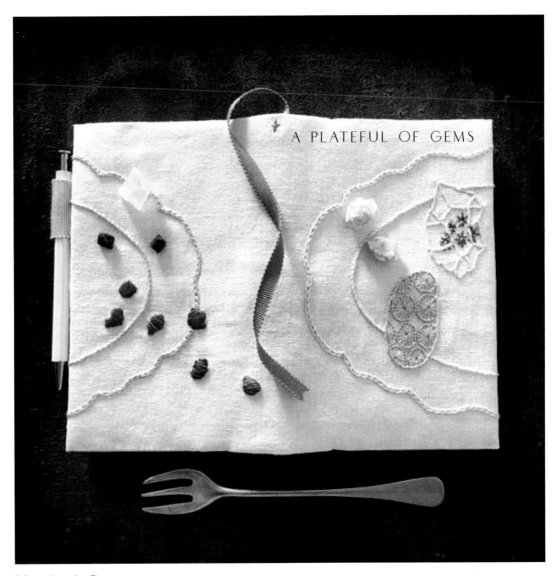

A PLATEFUL OF GEMS

Notebook Cover 🌰 instructions on page 68, 69

SENDING
A MESSAGE

Embroidered Card  instructions on page 67

BLUE LETTERS

Alphabet Sampler ✦ instructions on page 70

Yacht Tarts with Embroidered Flags instructions on page 71
(See the end of this book for a delicious tart recipe.)

Table Linens with European Motifs ❦ instructions on page 72

Far left, left: Yokohama Archives of History
Center: Yokohama Port Opening Memorial Hall

ADDING A PIECE OF
MARITIME HISTORY

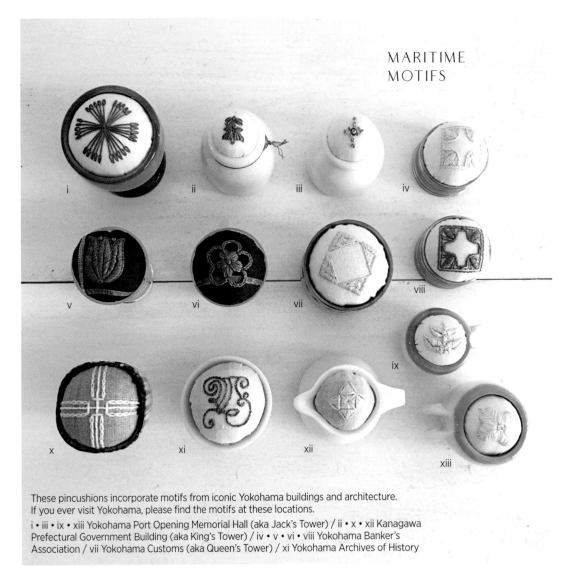

MARITIME
MOTIFS

These pincushions incorporate motifs from iconic Yokohama buildings and architecture.
If you ever visit Yokohama, please find the motifs at these locations.

i • iii • ix • xiii Yokohama Port Opening Memorial Hall (aka Jack's Tower) / ii • x • xii Kanagawa
Prefectural Government Building (aka King's Tower) / iv • v • vi • viii Yokohama Banker's
Association / vii Yokohama Customs (aka Queen's Tower) / xi Yokohama Archives of History

Pincushions Made from Flea Market Finds ● instructions on page 73

BLUE
SEASIDE
COFFEE
YOKOHAMA

Coasters ● instructions on page 74, 75

A SHELL
FOR
A DAY

Seashell Needle Books  instructions on page 61, 63

16

BISCUIT FROM THE SEA

Sea Biscuit Needle Books instructions on page 62, 63

SHELL DESIGNS

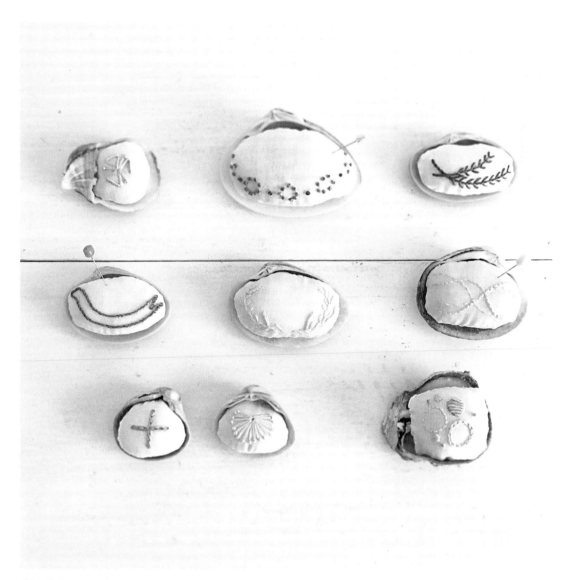

Shell Pincushions 🐚 instructions on page 76

A CONCH SHELL IN YOUR HAND

Conch Shell Scissors Holder 🐚 instructions on page 64, 65

BEYOND
THE
SEA
URCHIN

Sea Urchin Shell Pincushions 🐚 instructions on page 77

A SEA
GLASS
SPECIMEN
BOX

suna ni hikari ga

Sea Glass Sampler 🌰 instructions on page 78

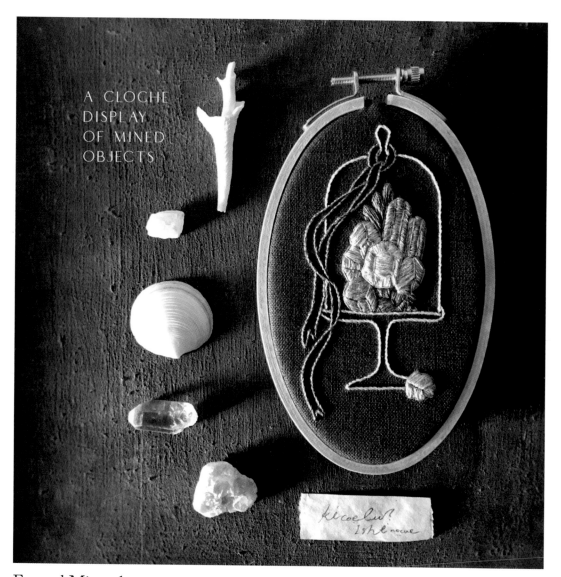

A CLOCHE
DISPLAY
OF MINED
OBJECTS

Framed Minerals 🏵 instructions on page 79

NOEL SWAG
MADE OF
BLUE PLANTS

Framed Winter Plants instructions on page 80

A FLUFFY COTTON FLOWER

Cotton Flower Pincushions ● instructions on page 80

SAILOR'S HAT
WITH RIBBON

Sea Voyage Bag I ❧ instructions on page 81, 85

GONDOLIER HATS

Sea Voyage Bag II  instructions on page 82, 85

WISHING
ON A
STARFISH

Sea Voyage Bag III ● instructions on page 83, 85

A SEABED ANCHOR

Sea Voyage Bag IV ● instructions on page 84, 85

Large Shawl with Acorn Designs instructions on page 86, 87

LUCKY
CHARMS
ON YOUR
BACK

I

II

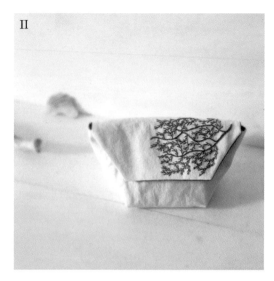

III

I   A sailor's collar
II   Between the waves, a sea fan
III Octopus meets ribbon

Ship Pouches ◈ instructions on page 88, 89

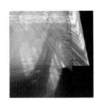   

Morning.
I toss dry food into the cats' bowl
I'm inspired to embroider the shape of their food.

As I hang the laundry outside, I pluck some flowering plants from the yard to
  decorate my room.
Perhaps I'll use the lemon from my garden as a motif for my next project.
I hope the lemons grow this year.

I boil water.
The "form" of the steam might make a cute embroidery design.
I pour a cup of tea. Today, it's an extra-hot black tea. Yesterday, I think I had coffee.

I head to my desk.
I choose thread colors.
The blue and white threads make me crave the sea.
The shade of blue I saw on the tile of an old building in Yokohama,
that's the blue I'm looking for.
I thread the needle.

Now it's time to embroider.

   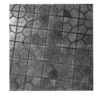

Straw Tote Cover instructions on page 90, 91

OCEAN
SYMBOLS

Embroidered Drawstring Bags ❧ instructions on page 92, 93

THE KEY TO UNLOCKING
THE OCEAN'S DOOR

Keychain Charms   instructions on page 94

YOU
AND
MISTLETOE

Embroidered Bracelet ❦ instructions on page 95

EMBROIDERY MATERIALS AND TOOLS

(a) Fabric

We recommend fabrics with a tighter weave. Before embroidering, soak the fabric in water for a few hours, then press with an iron while still damp to straighten the grain.

(b) Thread

In this book, we used these brands of embroidery thread: DMC, cosmo, Olympus and Appleton. Even if you don't have the same thread colors that are featured in the book, feel free to create your own colors by combining various threads you have on hand.

(c) Tracing kit

Tracing paper, craft carbon transfer paper, cellophane, tracing tool, paperweight. For the craft carbon transfer paper, try to find the water-soluble type. The gray color tends to be the most inconspicuous in cases where the markings don't fully disappear. Make sure to use a flat surface like a cutting mat for tracing designs.

(d) Pincushion

Having multiple pincushions to separate needles of different thicknesses is helpful. You could even make your own pincushions!

(e) (f) Scissors

Small thread-cutting scissors should have pointy tips and extra sharp blades. For cutting fabric, it's handy to have a larger pair of scissors as well as a small pair. A small pair of fabric scissors is useful for constructing little projects.

(g) Writing utensils

Tools for transferring the design onto the tracing paper include mechanical pencils, pens, pen-style eraser, ruler. To mark fabrics, use a water-soluble marking pen. When the design lines start to fade on the fabric, you can always re-draw them with the marking pen.

(h) Embroidery hoop

The easiest to use is typically about 4-6 inches (10-15 cm) in diameter. Wrap a piece of fabric around the inner hoop to cushion the fabric that will be embroidered. The wrapped inner hoop provides extra hold and prevents slippage of the fabric that will be embroidered.

HOW TO TRACE THE PATTERNS

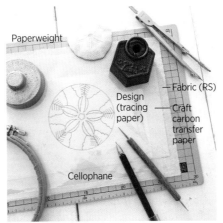

Paperweight

Fabric (RS)

Design (tracing paper)

Craft carbon transfer paper

Cellophane

1 Place in this order from bottom up: cutting board, fabric, craft carbon transfer paper, tracing paper with transferred design, cellophane. Secure the layers in place with a paperweight. As you trace the design, keep the desired composition and where the embroidery hoop will be positioned.

2 Trace the lines with a tracing tool. You will need to press extra firmly to transfer the lines through the carbon transfer paper onto the fabric. Periodically check that the lines are showing up on the fabric. If some of the lines are too faint or if there are certain sections you want to highlight as guidelines, use a fabric marking pen.

Tip Although the tracing step may feel mundane and tedious, the more clearly you trace the designs, the easier it will be to embroider, so it's important to take the time to do it right. Some types of carbon transfer paper will create permanent markings with heat-setting, so make sure to erase traced lines with water before applying an iron to the fabric. For small sections, use a damp cloth to erase the lines.

HOW TO USE #25 EMBROIDERY FLOSS

A skein of #25 embroidery thread is a single long thread looped multiple times. We will divide this long thread into eight equal parts for ease of use.

1 Maintaining the skein in its looped state, remove the labels. Check to ensure that the skein isn't tangled.

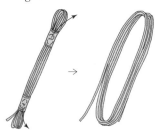

2 Without losing sight of the end of the thread, place the skein on top of a table and start unwinding it into a single thread.

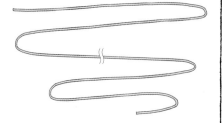

3 With the two ends together, fold the thread in half. Then fold in half again, and fold in half a third time. This will divide the thread into eight equal parts.

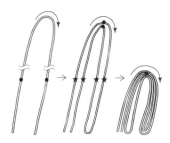

4 On the side where all of the thread is folded and looped, slip on the labels that were removed in step 1. Cut the looped thread on both sides. Since the label has information about the brand and thread color number that will be necessary if you need to buy additional skeins later, keep the label with the thread.

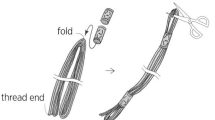

fold

thread end

Once you've divided the thread into eight parts…

You've now cut the skein into eight pieces of manageable length. Each of these thick pieces of thread is made up of six thinner strands.

1. Pull one thread from the bundle.
2. Pull apart the thinner strands one at a time. Each strand will be twisted, so you will need to straighten it as much as possible. Arrange the bundle of cut pieces neatly first to avoid a tangled mess as you pull the thread pieces out.
3. Pull apart the desired number of strands (the projects will specify 2-strand, 3-strand, etc.). Align the thread ends and trim to even out the length. When embroidering a small design, cut the strands to a shorter length to make embroidering easier.

BRANDS AND COLOR NUMBERS

Every embroidery thread label includes the brand and color number. Note that different brands may use the same color number but the colors themselves may be different based on the brand.

[Brand] cosmo, Olympus, DMC, etc.

[Color number]
For example:
DMC822 = Milk white (far right in photo)
Cosmo822 = Greenish beige
Olympus822 = does not exist
As you can see, cosmo and DMC use the same color number for completely different colors.

COMBINING THREAD COLORS

For example, you could take two strands of ivory embroidery thread and a strand of dark blue and combine them as one piece of thread; or combine milk white and snow white for subtle variations. Combining thread colors produces more depth and nuance and as you embroider, and different parts of the combined thread will emerge in the stitches. Enjoy the alchemy of mixing thread colors to create your own unique hues.

1 Prepare thread based on the "Color combination guide" section of the design. For instance, [a=D3033 ②+D930 ①] means to combine DMC3033 (Ivory) and DMC930 (Dark Blue) strands.

2 The circled number indicates the number of strands per color. D3033 ② →2 strands of Ivory / D930 ① → 1 strand of Dark Blue. You will combine the three strands to create a single thread.

3 Making sure that the strands do not get twisted or tangled, thread a needle with all three strands.

4 Explore different combinations such as blending similar colors or entirely different ones.

My Stitch Lesson Book

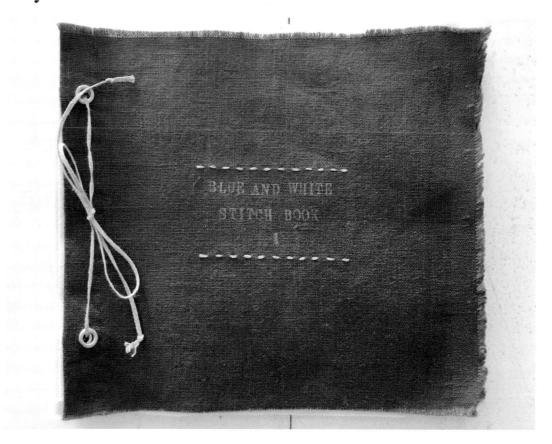

Design symbols and notations

Each design lists information in the following order: the embroidery stitch type • the first letter of the thread brand • color number • number of strands per thread (circled numbers indicate strand[s] per color).

For example, [Outline st. D169 ②] breaks down into the following:

- Outline st. = "Outline" indicates that an outline embroidery stitch is used, and "st." is the abbreviation for "stitch"
- D = is the first letter of the thread brand, which in this case is DMC (D=DMC, C=cosmo, O=Olympus, A=Appleton)
- 169 = color number (varies by brand)
- ② = 2 strands of designated color (②=2 strands, ③=3 strands)

When to combine thread colors: within the design, combined colors will be indicated by a lower case letter. For example: [Back st. a] means using a backstitch with combined color "a" which will be notated in the "Color combination guide" section.

Embroidery Stitches in This Book

(st. = abbreviation for "stitch")
※ ( ) indicates the stitch
order. For example, "1 out"
indicates that your first stitch
comes out/up through the
wrong side of the fabric.

Straight stitch

1 out
2 in

Running stitch

2 in
3 out
1 out
5 out
4 in

Outline stitch
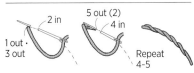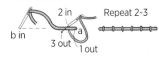
2 in
1 out ·
3 out
5 out (2)
4 in
Repeat
4-5

Back stitch
1 out 2 in
3 out
4 in (1)
3
5 out

Threaded back stitch

Whipped backstitch
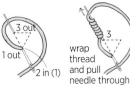

Couching stitch
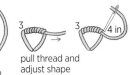
2 in
b in
3 out
a
1 out
Repeat 2-3

Fly stitch
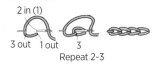
1 out
2 in
3 out
3
4 in

French knot stitch
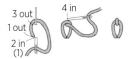
1 out
insert needle
tip into 2 while
pulling thread
2 in (1)
2 in

Bullion stitch triangle

3 out
1 out
2 in (1)
wrap
thread
and pull
needle through
3
3
3
4 in
pull thread and
adjust shape

Chain stitch
2 in (1)
3 out 1 out
3
Repeat 2-3

Lazy daisy stitch
3 out
1 out
2 in
(1)
4 in

Lazy daisy stitch
Straight stitch inside stitch

Lazy daisy stitch
Straight stitch over stitch

Feather stitch
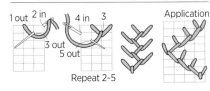
1 out
2 in
4 in
3
3 out
5 out
Repeat 2-5
Application

Blanket stitch (Buttonhole stitch)
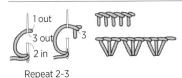
1 out
3 out
2 in
3
Repeat 2-3

Blanket stitch pinwheels
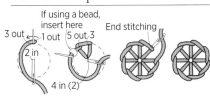
If using a bead,
insert here
3 out
1 out
5 out
3
2 in
4 in (2)
End stitching

Satin stitch

Start stitching from
the wide part
1 out 3 out
2 in
Once you reach the tip,
insert needle through
thread on underside
and complete
stitching the
other half
Seed st. (2-3 times)

Padded satin stitch
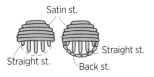
Satin st.
Straight st.
Straight st.
Back st.

Long & short stitch

2 in
3 out
1 out
Repeat 2-3 and fill the design

Lesson 1 Running stitch and Straight stitch

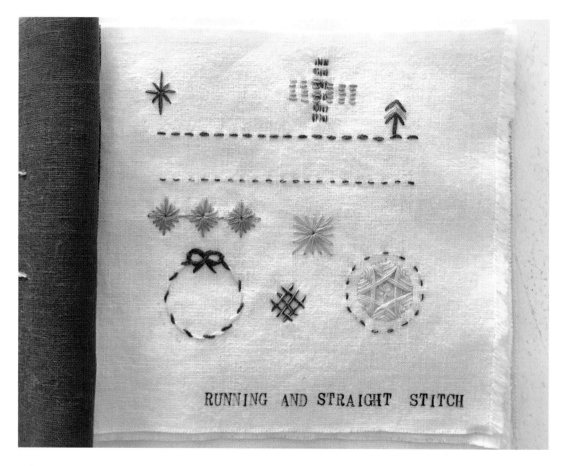

RUNNING AND STRAIGHT STITCH

T i p Try to follow the natural twisting direction of the thread as you stitch. This way, the simpler the stitch, the cleaner the finish. For circular designs, stitch in the same direction all the way around.

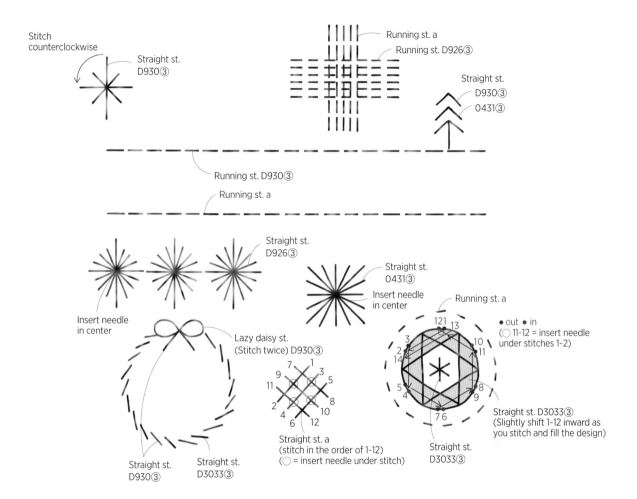

Stitch counterclockwise

Straight st. D930③

Running st. a
Running st. D926③

Straight st. D930③
0431③

Running st. D930③

Running st. a

Straight st. D926③

Straight st. 0431③

Insert needle in center

Running st. a

121 13
3 10
2 11
14
● out ● in
(○ 11-12 = insert needle under stitches 1-2)
5 8
4 9
7 6

Straight st. D3033③
(Slightly shift 1-12 inward as you stitch and fill the design)

Straight st. D3033③

Insert needle in center

Lazy daisy st. (Stitch twice) D930③

7 1
9 3 5
11
2 8
4 10
6 12

Straight st. a
(stitch in the order of 1-12)
(○ = insert needle under stitch)

Straight st. D930③
Straight st. D3033③

Embroidery thread colors

※ The numbers within [ ] represent DMC corresponding color numbers.

DMC ● 926 [Dark Aqua] / ● 930 (Dark Blue) / ● 3033 (Ivory)
Olympus ● 431 [3023] (Soft Khaki)

Color combination guide

a=D930 ②+D3033 ①

※ Add the circled numbers for the total number of strands per thread piece. Example: ②+①= 3-strand thread

※ D = DMC

Lesson 2 Back stitch

Tip For optimal back stitching, always insert the needle in the previous hole for an evenly connected line. For curved lines, use smaller stitches and make sure to start off with a smaller stitch. You could also change up the stitch width for a charming effect.

※ The numbers within [   ] represent DMC corresponding color numbers.

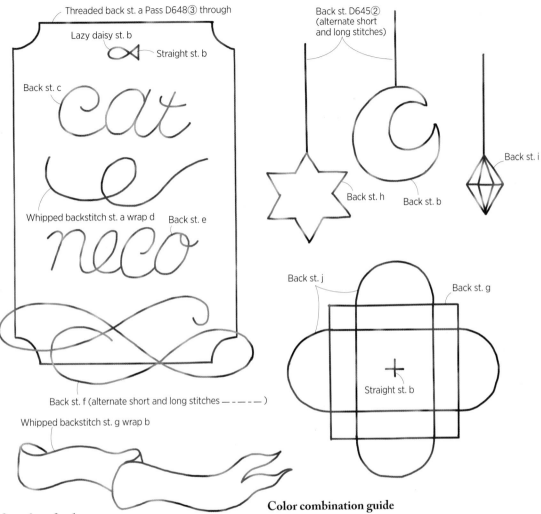

Threaded back st. a Pass D648③ through

Lazy daisy st. b

Straight st. b

Back st. c

Back st. D645② (alternate short and long stitches)

Back st. i

Back st. h

Back st. b

Whipped backstitch st. a wrap d

Back st. e

Back st. j

Back st. g

Straight st. b

Back st. f (alternate short and long stitches – – – – –)

Whipped backstitch st. g wrap b

Embroidery thread colors

※ The numbers within [ ] represent DMC corresponding color numbers.

DMC ● 169 (Smoke Blue) / ● 645 (Olive) / ● 648 (Pearl Gray) / ● 822 (Milk White) / ● 926 (Dark Aqua) / ● 3033 (Ivory)

Olympus ● 413 [646] (Gray / ● 430 [3024] (Silver Gray)

● 3043 [3768] (Saxe Blue)

Color combination guide

a=D3033 ②+D822 ①/ b =D169 ②+O3043 ①/ c =D169 ② +O413 ①/ d =D648 ②+O413 ①/ e =O413 ②+D169 ①/ f=D169 ②+D926 ②/ g =D822 ②+O430 ①/ h =O3043 ②+D645 ①/ i =D169 ②+D926 ①/ j =O430 ②+D822 ①

※ Add the circled numbers for the total number of strands per thread piece. Example: ②+①=3-strand thread, ②+②=4-strand thread

※ D = DMC, O = Olympus

back

T i p Sometimes the threads on the underside will be visible on the right side of the fabric, so the threads will need to be tidied up on the underside. Since the underside is visible for projects like handkerchiefs and table linens, pay particular attention to tidying up the threads.

STARTING AND ENDING STITCHES

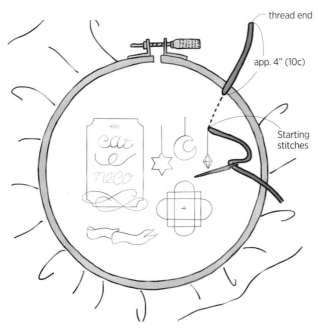

thread end

app. 4" (10c)

Starting stitches

Starting stitches

Lines … (back st., outline st., etc.)

- Insert needle a little bit away from the starting point, and leaving a thread tail of about 4" (10 cm) on the right side, start embroidering.
- Press down on the thread tail as you start embroidering, and after two or three stitches, the tail should be secured.
- Once you've completed the embroidery, pull the tail to the wrong side and finish using the method in the "Ending stitches" section.

Surface stitches … (satin st., long and short st., etc.)

- In a section that will be hidden beneath the surface stitches, form 2 ~ 3 seed stitches and once the thread is secured, start embroidering.

Ending stitches

- For lines and surface stitches, loop or wrap thread around underside stitches 2 ~ 3 times and clip thread.
- Make sure that the stitches on the right side are not affected as you wrap the stitches on the underside.

Isolated stitches

- When making a single French knot or an isolated straight stitch far removed from the main design, knot the thread at the beginning and end of the stitch.
- If there is a cluster of underside stitches nearby, however, wrap the thread in the cluster and then begin or end stitching.

(WS)

(WS)

Lesson 3 Outline stitch

Tip Outline stitches are ideal for curved lines. You can create beautiful curves with small, delicate stitches. Using a thicker, 5- or 6-strand thread lends itself to a rope-like effect that works well for marine-themed designs.

Outline st. d

French knot st. d
(wrap 3 times)

Outline st. a

Outline st. next to
each other

Outline st. e

Straight st. b

Lazy daisy st. f

Outline st. f

Outline st. c

Outline st. g

Embroidery Thread Colors

※ The numbers within [ ] represent DMC corresponding
   color numbers.

DMC ● 169 (Smoke Blue) / ● 413 (Blue Gray) / ● 535
(Steel Gray) / ● 646 (Khaki) / ● 647 (Silver Khaki) /
● 648 (Pearl Gray) / ● 928 (Baby Sky Blue) / ● 3024
(Snow White) / ● 3033 (Ivory)

cosmo ● 151 [3024] (Cold White) / ● 366 [3782] (Ecru)

Olympus ● 3043 [3768] (Saxe Blue)

Color combination guide

a =D647 ①+D648 ①+D928 ①/ b =D648 ②+D647 ①/ c
=D169 ②+D648 ①/ d =D3024 ①+D3033 ①/ e =O3043
②+D413 ①/ f =D646 ②+D535 ①/ g =C151 ②+C366 ②

※ Add the circled numbers for the total number of strands
   per thread piece. Example: ②+①=3-strand thread

※ D = DMC, C = cosmo, O = Olympus

Lesson 4 Chain stitch

Tip The aim is to form even-sized stitches for each chain link. When filling the surface with chain stitches, aligning the stitches for each row creates the appearance of knitted stitches.

Enlarge design by 125%

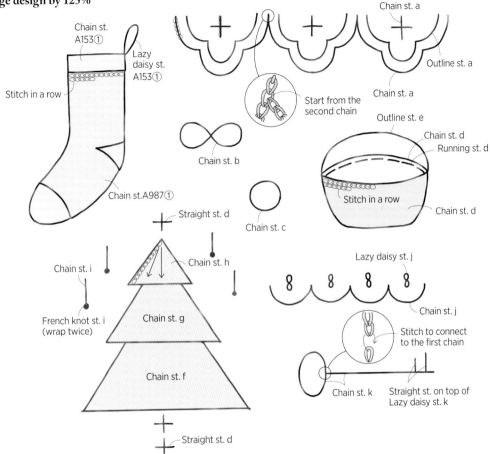

Chain st. A153①
Lazy daisy st. A153①
Stitch in a row
Chain st. A987①
Chain st. a
Outline st. a
Start from the second chain
Chain st. a
Outline st. e
Chain st. d
Running st. d
Chain st. b
Stitch in a row
Chain st. d
Straight st. d
Chain st. c
Chain st. i
Chain st. h
French knot st. i (wrap twice)
Chain st. g
Chain st. f
Lazy daisy st. j
Chain st. j
Stitch to connect to the first chain
Chain st. k
Straight st. on top of Lazy daisy st. k
Straight st. d

Embroidery Thread Colors

※ The numbers within [ ] represent DMC corresponding color numbers.

Appleton ◯ 153 (Horizon Blue) / ● 987 (White Smoke)
DMC ● 535 (Steel Gray) / ◯ 613 (Off-White) / ◯ 644 (Khaki White) / ● 647 (Silver Khaki) / ◯ 648 (Pearl Gray) / ● 926 (Dark Aqua) / ◯ 3033 (Ivory) / ● 3768 (Iron Blue)
cosmo ◯ 151 [3024] (Cold White) / ◯ 366 [3782] (Ecru) / ● 368 [611] (Light Beige)
Olympus ◯ 431 [3023] (Soft Khaki)

Color combination guide

a =C151 ②+D613 ①/ b =D926 ②+D647 ①/ c =D613 ② +D644 ①/ d =D3768 ②+C368 ①/ e =D3768 ④+C368 ② / f =D644 ②+O431 ①/ g =O431 ②+D644 ①/ h =C366 ②+O431 ①/ i =D644 ②+D613 ①/ j =D644 ①+D648 ①+ D3033 ①/ k =D3768 ②+D535 ①

※ Add the circled numbers for the total number of strands per thread piece. Example: ②+①=3-strand thread, ④+②=6-strand thread

※ D = DMC, C = cosmo, O = Olympus

Lesson 5 Lazy Daisy stitch

LAZY DAISY STITCH

Tip With the rounded shape of flower petals in mind, keep the stitches small to yield this cute design. For variety, lengthen the securing straight stitch at the base of the elliptical shape, or attach fly stitches to configure little fishies.

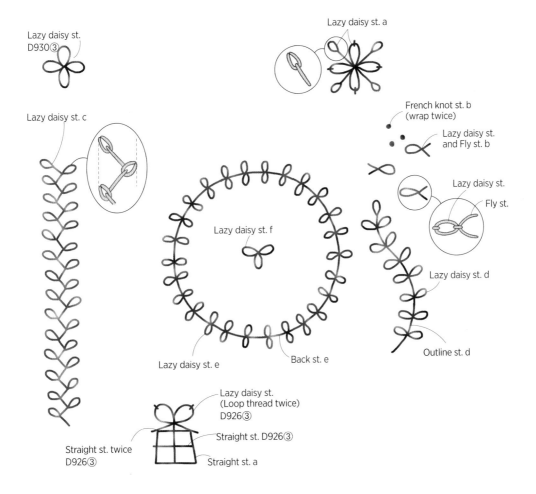

Lazy daisy st.
D930③

Lazy daisy st. a

French knot st. b
(wrap twice)

Lazy daisy st.
and Fly st. b

Lazy daisy st. c

Lazy daisy st.

Fly st.

Lazy daisy st. f

Lazy daisy st. d

Lazy daisy st. e

Back st. e

Outline st. d

Lazy daisy st.
(Loop thread twice)
D926③

Straight st. D926③

Straight st. twice
D926③

Straight st. a

Embroidery Thread Colors

※ The numbers within [ ] represent DMC corresponding color numbers.

DMC ● 926 (Dark Aqua) / ● 930 (Dark Blue) / ● 3033 (Ivory)
cosmo ● 366 [3782] (Ecru)
Olympus ● 431 [3023] (Soft Khaki)

Color combination guide

a =O431 ②+C366 ①/ b =D3033 ②+D926 ①/ c =O431 ②+D926 ①/ d =D926 ①+D930 ①/ e =D3033 ①+O431 ①/f =D3033 ②+O431 ①

※ Add the circled numbers for the total number of strands per thread piece. Example: ②+①=3-strand thread, ①+①=2-strand thread

※ D = DMC, C = cosmo, O = Olympus

Lesson 6 French Knot stitch

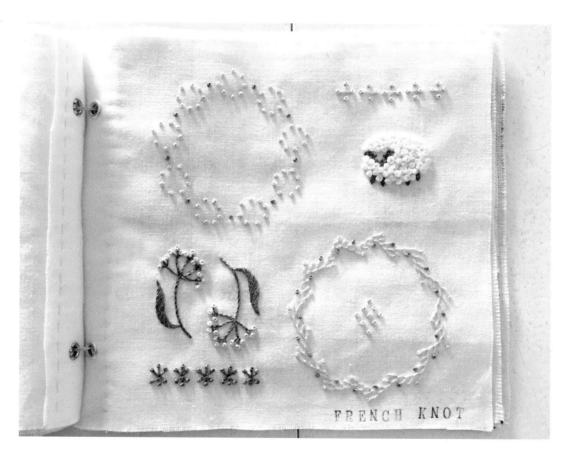

Tip Arrange the knot in a pleasing way before inserting the needle and pulling the thread to the underside. Hold the knot as you pull the thread slowly. Rushing will result in tangled threads, so take your time.

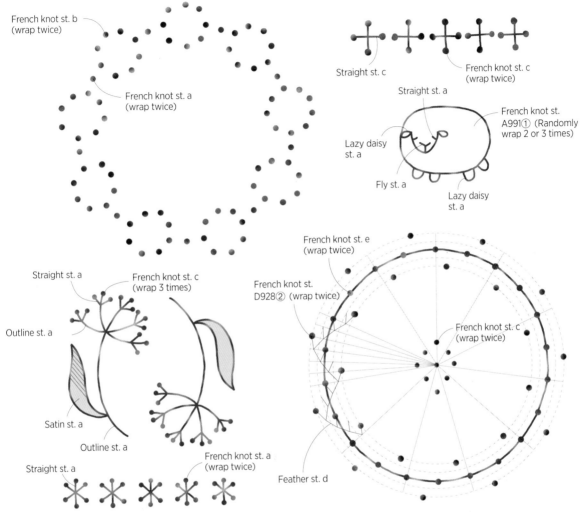

French knot st. b
(wrap twice)

French knot st. a
(wrap twice)

Straight st. c

French knot st. c
(wrap twice)

Straight st. a

French knot st.
A991① (Randomly
wrap 2 or 3 times)

Lazy daisy
st. a

Fly st. a

Lazy daisy
st. a

Straight st. a

French knot st. c
(wrap 3 times)

Outline st. a

Satin st. a

Outline st. a

Straight st. a

French knot st. a
(wrap twice)

French knot st. e
(wrap twice)

French knot st.
D928② (wrap twice)

French knot st. c
(wrap twice)

Feather st. d

Embroidery Thread Colors

※ The numbers within [ ] represent DMC corresponding color numbers.

Appleton ● 991 (White)

DMC ● 613 (Off-White) / ● 712 (Warm White) / ● 926 (Dark Aqua) / ● 928 (Baby Sky Blue) / ● 3033 (Ivory) / ● 3768 (Iron Blue)

cosmo ● 890 [648] (White Gray)

Olympus ● 421 [822] (Pearl Gray)

Color combination guide

a =D926 ②+D3768 ①/ b =C890 ②+O421 ①/
c =D613 ②+D3033 ①/ d =D712 ②+D3033 ①/
e =D3768 ①+D926 ①

※ Add the circled numbers for the total number of strands per thread piece.
Example: ②+①=3-strand thread,
①+①=2-strand thread

※ D = DMC, C = cosmo, O = Olympus

Lesson 7 Blanket stitch

T i p This versatile stitch can decorate fabric edges, form an interesting ring formation, secure appliqué pieces and so much more. In every case, take the time to create stitches of equal length that are evenly spaced apart for best results. To incorporate beads, slip on the bead before scooping up the fabric for the next stitch. Make sure to use a needle that is thin enough to fit in the bead opening.

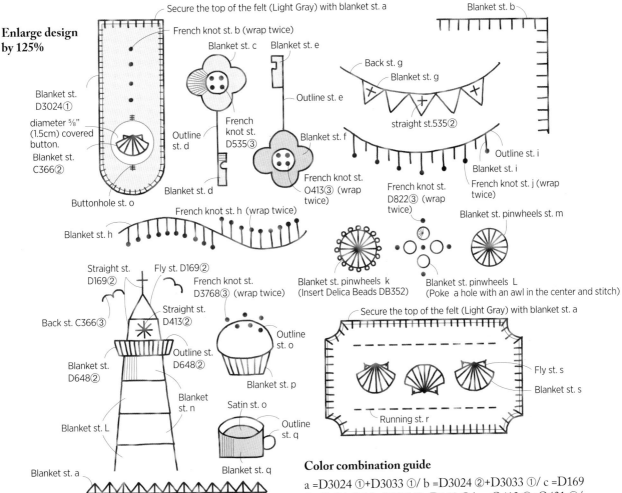

Enlarge design by 125%

Secure the top of the felt (Light Gray) with blanket st. a

French knot st. b (wrap twice)

Blanket st. c

Blanket st. e

Blanket st. b

Back st. g

Blanket st. g

Blanket st. D3024①

diameter ⅝" (1.5cm) covered button.

Blanket st. C366②

Outline st. d

Outline st. e

French knot st. D535③

Blanket st. f

straight st.535②

Outline st. i

Blanket st. i

French knot st. j (wrap twice)

Buttonhole st. o

Blanket st. d

French knot st. O413③ (wrap twice)

French knot st. D822③ (wrap twice)

French knot st. h (wrap twice)

Blanket st. h

Blanket st. pinwheels st. m

Blanket st. pinwheels k (Insert Delica Beads DB352)

Blanket st. pinwheels L (Poke a hole with an awl in the center and stitch)

Secure the top of the felt (Light Gray) with blanket st. a

Straight st. D169②

Fly st. D169②

French knot st. D3768③ (wrap twice)

Straight st. D413②

Back st. C366③

Blanket st. D648②

Outline st. D648②

Outline st. o

Fly st. s

Blanket st. s

Blanket st. n

Satin st. o

Blanket st. L

Blanket st. a

Blanket st. q

Outline st. q

Running st. r

Blanket st. p

Embroidery Thread Colors

※ The numbers within [ ] represent DMC corresponding color numbers.

DMC ● 169 (Smoke Blue) / ● 413 (Blue Gray) / ● 535 (Steel Gray) / 613 (Off-White) / ● 648 (Pearl Gray) / 822 (Milk White) / ● 926 (Dark Aqua) / 3024 (Snow White) / 3033 (Ivory) / ● 3768 (Iron Blue)

cosmo 151 [3024] (Cold White) / ● 366 [3782] (Ecru)

Olympus ● 413 [646] (Gray) / 421 [822] (Pearl Gray) / ● 431 [3023] (Soft Khaki)

Color combination guide

a =D3024 ①+D3033 ①/ b =D3024 ②+D3033 ①/ c =D169 ②+O431 ①/ d =D535 ②+D169 ①/ e =O413 ②+O431 ①/ f =3033 ②+O431 ①/ g =D3768 ②+D535 ①/ h =D535 ②+D926 ①/ i =D648 ②+O431 ①/ j =D648 ②+O421 ①/ k =169 ①+D648 ①/ L =D169 ②+D926 ①/ m =D3768 ②+D169 ①/ n =O421 ②+O431 ①/ o =C366 ②+D822 ①/ p =D169 ①+O431 ①/ q =D3768 ②+D169 ①/ r =D613 ②+ C151 ①/ s =D613 ①+C151 ①

※ Add the circled numbers for the total number of strands per thread piece. Example: ②+①=3-strand thread, ②+①=3-strand thread

※ D = DMC, C = cosmo, O = Olympus

Stitch Lesson Book

See photos on pages 42–59

Materials

Linen for front and back covers: [Blue] 12" x 12"
   (30cm x 30cm) 1 each
Linen for stitch design pages: [White] 12" x 12"
   (30cm x 30cm) 1 per stitch design
String: approximately 39¼" (1m)
Eyelet: 2 sets

Alphabet stamp
Fabric ink stamp pad

Finished dimensions (metric measurements are more
   precise)
Approximately 6¼" x 7" (16cm x 18cm).

1. Embroider on prepared fabric that is slightly
   larger than needed.

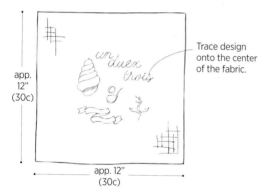

app.
12"
(30c)

app. 12"
(30c)

Trace design
onto the center
of the fabric.

2. Cut to designated stitch book size.

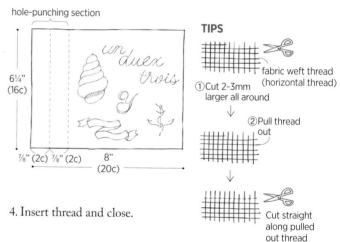

hole-punching section

6¼"
(16c)

⅞" (2c)   ⅞" (2c)   8"
                      (20c)

TIPS

fabric weft thread
(horizontal thread)

①Cut 2-3mm
larger all around

②Pull thread
out

Cut straight
along pulled
out thread

3. Stamp and make holes.

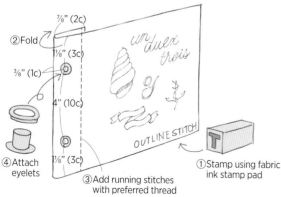

②Fold

⅞" (2c)

1⅛" (3c)

⅜" (1c)

4" (10c)

1⅛" (3c)

④Attach
eyelets

③Add running stitches
with preferred thread

OUTLINE STITCH

①Stamp using fabric
ink stamp pad

4. Insert thread and close.

BLUE AND WHITE
STITCH BOOK
1

Running st.   Stamp

Repeat steps 1-3
for front cover with
blue fabric.

Seashell Needle Books

See photo on page 16 / instructions on page 63

Embroidery thread colors

※ The numbers within [ ] represent DMC corresponding color numbers.

i DMC ○ 3866 (Whitewash) / Olympus ○ 421[822] (Pearl Gray)

ii DMC ● 647 (Silver Khaki) / ● 926 (Dark Aqua)
   cosmo ● 890 [648] (White Gray)

iii DMC ○ 613 (Off-White) / ○ 712 (Warm White)

iv DMC ○ 3866 (Whitewash) / cosmo ● 890 [648] (White Gray)
   Olympus ○ 421 [822] (Pearl Gray)

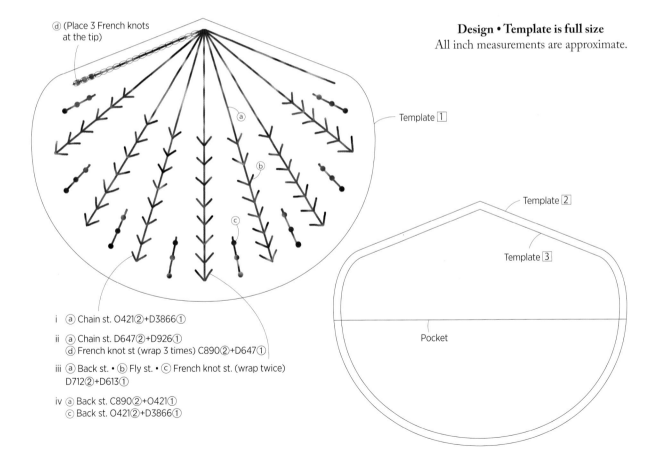

ⓓ (Place 3 French knots at the tip)

ⓐ ⓑ ⓒ

Template ①

Design • Template is full size
All inch measurements are approximate.

Template ②

Template ③

Pocket

i ⓐ Chain st. O421②+D3866①

ii ⓐ Chain st. D647②+D926①
   ⓓ French knot st (wrap 3 times) C890②+D647①

iii ⓐ Back st. • ⓑ Fly st. • ⓒ French knot st. (wrap twice)
    D712②+D613①

iv ⓐ Back st. C890②+O421①
   ⓒ Back st. O421②+D3866①

Sea Biscuit Needle Books

See photo on page 17 / instructions on page 63

Embroidery thread colors

※ The numbers within [ ] represent DMC corresponding color numbers.

i   DMC ● 926 (Dark Aqua) / ● 3768 (Iron Blue) / ◐ 3866 (Whitewash)
    Olympus ◐ 421 [822] (Pearl Gray)
ii DMC ◐ 613 (Off-White) / ◯ 712 (Warm White) / ◐ 3033 (Ivory)
iii DMC ● 647 (Silver Khaki) / ● 926 (Dark Aqua)
    cosmo ● 366 [3782] (Ecru) / Olympus ● 431 [3023] (Soft Khaki)

Design • Template is full size
All inch measurements are approximate.

How to stitch the center pentagon

② ① ⑤
③ ④

In the order of ①-⑤,
continuously shift the stitches
inward to fill the design

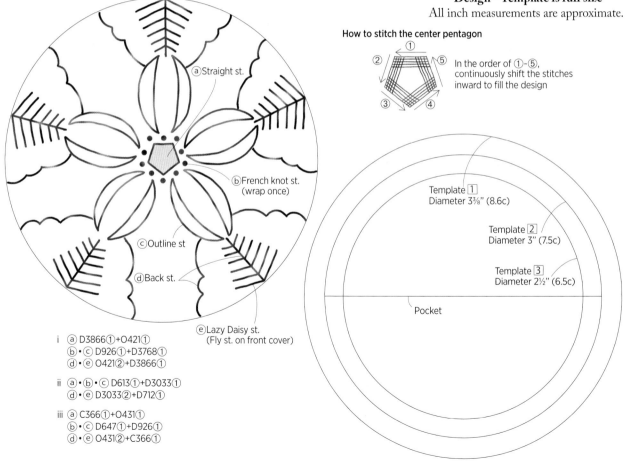

ⓐ Straight st.

ⓑ French knot st.
(wrap once)

ⓒ Outline st

ⓓ Back st.

ⓔ Lazy Daisy st.
(Fly st. on front cover)

Template ①
Diameter 3⅜" (8.6c)

Template ②
Diameter 3" (7.5c)

Template ③
Diameter 2½" (6.5c)

Pocket

i   ⓐ D3866①+O421①
    ⓑ•ⓒ D926①+D3768①
    ⓓ•ⓔ O421②+D3866①

ii ⓐ•ⓑ•ⓒ D613①+D3033①
    ⓓ•ⓔ D3033②+D712①

iii ⓐ C366①+O431①
    ⓑ•ⓒ D647①+D926①
    ⓓ•ⓔ O431②+C366①

Seashell Needle Books / Sea Biscuit Needle Books

See photos on pages 16-17

Materials (same for both)

Fabric for outer • lining: White linen 6" x 6" (15cm x 15cm), 1 each

Fusible interfacing: 6" x 6" (15cm x 15cm), 2 pieces

Cardboard: 4" x 4" (10cm x 10cm), 2 pieces

Quilt batting: 8" x 8" (20cm x 20cm), 1 piece

Gray felt (for backing): 8" x 8" (20cm x 20cm), 1 piece

Beige felt (for pages): 8" x 8" (20cm x 20cm), 1 piece

¼" (0.6cm)- wide ribbon: 8" (20cm), 2 pieces

1⅜" (3.5cm)- wide grosgrain ribbon: 2" (5cm), 1 piece

Finished dimensions (metric measurements are more precise)

Shell needle book: 3" x 3⅔" (7.5cm x 9.3cm)

Biscuit needle book: 3⅜" (8.6cm) diameter

1. Embroider fabric and prepare parts (make and use the "templates ①•②• ③" in the design).

Template c

[Front cover] 1 piece   [Back cover] 1 piece

③Add ⅞" (2cm) seam allowance and cut

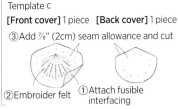

②Embroider felt   ①Attach fusible interfacing

[Cardboard, Quilt batting (small)]

2 pieces each

Template ②

[Felt]
Pages: 2 pieces,
Backing: 2 pieces

[Pocket]
1 piece
Use pinking shears to cut top edge

Felt

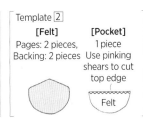

Template ③

[Quilt batting (small)]
2 pieces

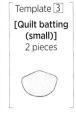

2. Sew along the edges of the front and back with gathering stitches

¼" (0.5c)   seam allowance ⅞" (2c)

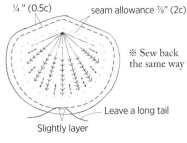

※ Sew back the same way

Leave a long tail

Slightly layer

3. Layer the parts

Quilt batting (small)

Cardboard

Quilt batting (large)

Front (WS)

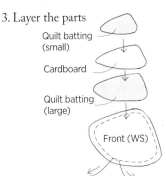

4. Arrange the shape

※ Assemble the back the same way

Layer and sew to gather fabric

(WS)

Sew to secure and enhance the shape of the front

Front piece   ↓   Back piece

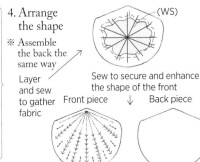

5. Attach pocket

Attach pocket (1 only)

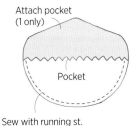

Pocket

Sew with running st.

6. Make the pages

app. ⅜" (1c)   Secure with blanket st.

Felt for pages

For the Sea Biscuit, secure the left edge

Lining fabric with pocket attached

7. Assemble

Front piece (WS)

①Sew on ¼" (0.6 cm)- wide ribbon

②Sew on 1⅜" (3.5 cm)- wide ribbon

Back piece (WS)

app. ⅜" (1c)   app. ¼" (0.5c)

Lining fabric

Felt with pocket

③Lining fabric to stitch onto the wrong side of cover

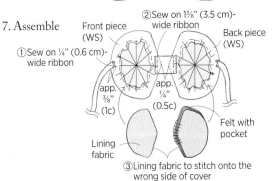

Conch Shell Scissors Holder

See photo on page 20

Materials

A. Outer fabric: White linen 8" x 8" (20cm x 20cm) 1 piece
Lightweight fusible interfacing: 6" x 6" (15cm x 15cm) 1 piece
Lining fabric: Navy cotton 8" x 8" (20cm x 20cm) 1 piece

B. Outer fabric: Navy cotton 8" x 8" (20cm x 20cm) 1 piece
Heavyweight fusible interfacing: 6" x 6" (15cm x 15cm) 1 piece
Lining fabric: White canvas 8" x 8" (20cm x 20cm) 1 piece

Wool batting

Finished dimensions (metric measurements are more precise)
5" x 3" (12.5cm x 7.5cm)

Embroidery thread colors

※ The numbers within [ ] represent DMC corresponding color numbers.

DMC ◔ 3866 (Whitewash) / cosmo ● 890 [648] (White Gray)

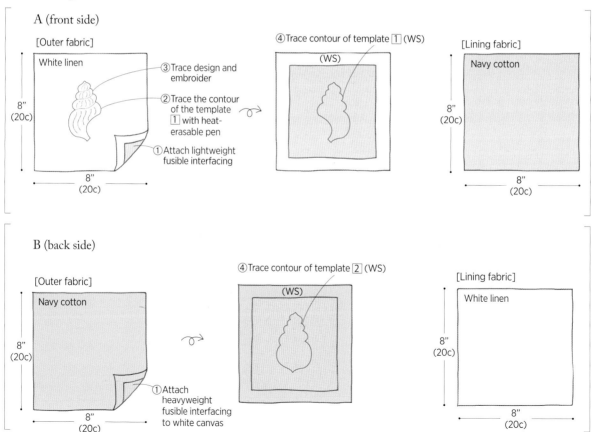

A (front side)

[Outer fabric]

White linen

③ Trace design and embroider

② Trace the contour of the template 1 with heat-erasable pen

① Attach lightweight fusible interfacing

8" (20c)

8" (20c)

④ Trace contour of template 1 (WS)

(WS)

[Lining fabric]

Navy cotton

8" (20c)

8" (20c)

B (back side)

[Outer fabric]

Navy cotton

① Attach heavyweight fusible interfacing to white canvas

8" (20c)

8" (20c)

④ Trace contour of template 2 (WS)

(WS)

[Lining fabric]

White linen

8" (20c)

8" (20c)

1. Place the outer and lining fabrics of A (front side) with right sides together

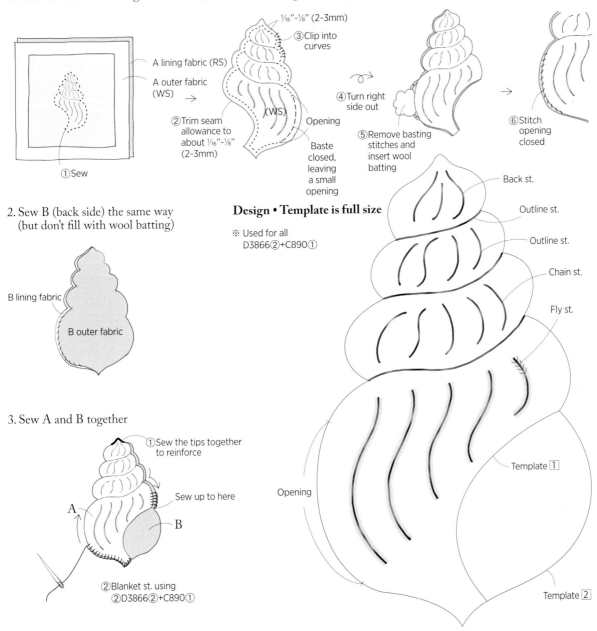

A lining fabric (RS)

A outer fabric (WS) →

① Sew

② Trim seam allowance to about 1/16"~1/8" (2-3mm)

1/16"~1/8" (2-3mm)

③ Clip into curves

(WS)

Opening

Baste closed, leaving a small opening

④ Turn right side out

⑤ Remove basting stitches and insert wool batting

⑥ Stitch opening closed

2. Sew B (back side) the same way (but don't fill with wool batting)

B lining fabric

B outer fabric

3. Sew A and B together

① Sew the tips together to reinforce

Sew up to here

A

B

② Blanket st. using ②D3866②+C890①

Design • Template is full size

※ Used for all D3866②+C890①

Back st.

Outline st.

Outline st.

Chain st.

Fly st.

Template 1

Template 2

Opening

Cloth with Appliquéd Anchor

See photo on page 6

Embroidery thread colors (Cloth with Appliquéd Anchor)

※ The numbers within [ ] represent DMC corresponding color numbers.

DMC 613 (Off-White) / 3768 (Iron Blue)

cosmo 151 [3024] (Cold White)

Olympus 3043 [3768] (Saxe Blue)

Hand Towel Embroidery

See photo on page 7

Embroidery thread colors (Hand Towel Embroidery)

※ The numbers within [ ] represent DMC corresponding color numbers.

DMC 535 (Steel Gray) / 613 (Off-White) / 712 (Warm White) / 3768 (Iron Blue)

Design • Template is full size

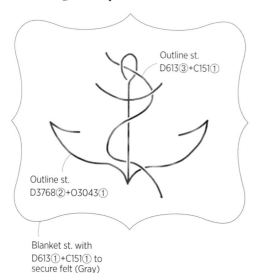

Outline st.
D613③+C151①

Outline st.
D3768②+O3043①

Blanket st. with
D613①+C151① to
secure felt (Gray)

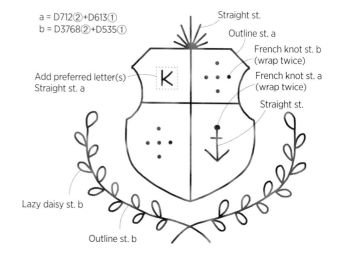

a = D712②+D613①
b = D3768②+D535①

Add preferred letter(s)
Straight st. a

Lazy daisy st. b

Outline st. b

Straight st.

Outline st. a

French knot st. b
(wrap twice)

French knot st. a
(wrap twice)

Straight st.

Embroidered Card

See photo on page 9

Materials

Paper for card: 3⅝" x 2⅛" (9.2cm x 5.5cm) 2 pieces

Finished dimensions (metric measurements are more precise)
3⅝" x 2⅛" (9.2cm x 5.5cm)

Embroidery thread colors

※ The numbers within [ ] represent DMC corresponding color numbers.

DMC 613 (Off-White) / 3033 (Ivory) / Diamant 168 (Silver)

Design • Template is full size

※ ● indicates where to poke holes with a thin needle to prepare for paper embroidery

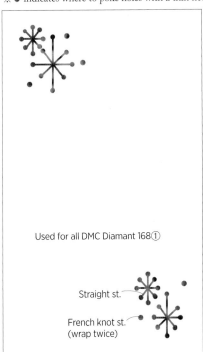

Used for all DMC Diamant 168①

Straight st.

French knot st.
(wrap twice)

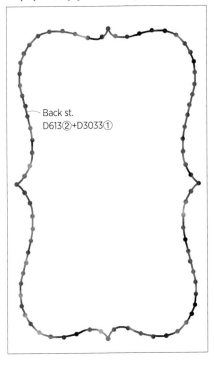

Back st.
D613②+D3033①

1. Copy the design onto tracing paper, then poke holes in the card paper

Poke holes in card paper with a thin needle

Tracing paper

Card paper

Lay a thin towel underneath

2. Embroider using the holes

3. On the back, glue a same-size piece of card paper

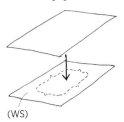

(WS)

Notebook Cover

See photo on page 8

Materials

White linen: 12" x 22" (30cm x 56cm)

¼" (0.6cm)- wide grosgrain ribbon: 7½" (19cm)

1" (2.5cm)- wide grosgrain ribbon: 3" (7.5cm)

Finished dimensions (closed)

(metric measurements are more precise)

5¾" x 4" (14.5cm x 10cm)

Embroidery thread colors (Cloth with Appliquéd Anchor)

※ The numbers within [ ] represent DMC corresponding color numbers.

DMC 169 (Smoke Blue) / 413 (Blue Gray) / 613 (Off-White) / 644 (Khaki White) / 645 (Olive) / 647 (Silver Khaki) / 648 (Pearl Gray) / 822 (Milk White) / 926 (Dark Aqua) / 928 (Baby Sky Blue) / 930 (Dark Blue) / 3024 (Snow White) / 3033 (Ivory) / 3750 (Midnight Blue) / 3768 (Iron Blue) / 3866 (Whitewash)

cosmo 890 [648] (White Gray)

Olympus 354 [322] (Light Sky) / 430 [3024] (Silver Gray)

Color combination guide

a=D413 ①+D645 ① +D3768 ①/ b=D169 ①+D413 ①+D3768 ①/ c=D930 ①+D3750 ①+D3768 ①/ d=C890 ②+D644 ①/ e=D613 ①+D648 ①+D3033 ①/ f=D648 ①+D3033 ①/ g=D3768 ② +D169 ①/ h=D3866 ② +D3024 ②/ i=D647 ① +D926 ① +O354 ①/ j=O430 ① D644 ①+D648 ①+D928 ①/ k=D822 ②+D3024 ①

※ Add the circled numbers for the total number of strands per thread piece.
   Example: ②+①=3-strand thread, ①+①+①=3-strand thread

※ D = DMC, C = cosmo, O = Olympus

Enlarge design by 200%

[Finished dimensions • Design]

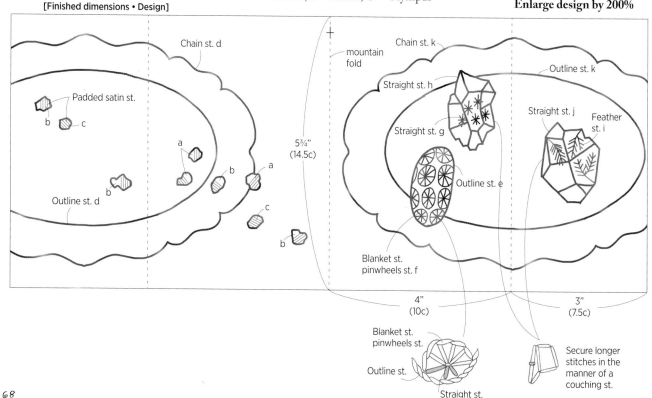

Chain st. d

Padded satin st.

b — c

a

b — a

Outline st. d

b

c

b

mountain fold

5¾" (14.5c)

Chain st. k

Straight st. h

Straight st. g

Outline st. k

Straight st. j

Feather st. i

Outline st. e

Blanket st. pinwheels st. f

4" (10c)

3" (7.5c)

Blanket st. pinwheels st.

Outline st.

Straight st.

Secure longer stitches in the manner of a couching st.

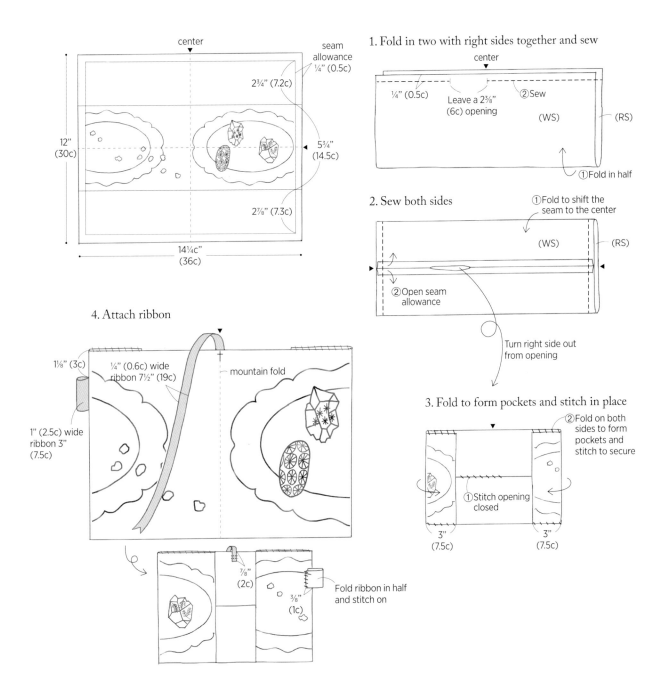

center

seam
allowance
¼" (0.5c)

2¾" (7.2c)

12"
(30c)

5¾"
(14.5c)

2⅞" (7.3c)

14¼c"
(36c)

1. Fold in two with right sides together and sew

center

¼" (0.5c)

Leave a 2⅜"
(6c) opening

②Sew

(WS)

(RS)

①Fold in half

2. Sew both sides

①Fold to shift the
seam to the center

(WS)

(RS)

②Open seam
allowance

Turn right side out
from opening

3. Fold to form pockets and stitch in place

②Fold on both
sides to form
pockets and
stitch to secure

①Stitch opening
closed

3"
(7.5c)

3"
(7.5c)

4. Attach ribbon

1⅛" (3c)

¼" (0.6c) wide
ribbon 7½" (19c)

mountain fold

1" (2.5c) wide
ribbon 3"
(7.5c)

⅞"
(2c)

⅜"
(1c)

Fold ribbon in half
and stitch on

Alphabet Sampler

Enlarge design by 125%

See photo on page 10

Embroidery thread colors

※ The numbers within [ ] represent DMC corresponding color numbers.

DMC 647 (Silver Khaki) / 926 (Dark Aqua) / 927 (Aqua) / 928 (Baby Sky Blue) / 930 (Dark Blue) / 3033 (Ivory) / 3768 (Iron Blue)

Olympus 423 [646] (Khaki Gray) / 431 [3023] (Soft Khaki) / 3043 [3768] (Saxe Blue)

Color combination guide

a=D927 ②+O431 ①/ b=O3043 ②+D647 ①/ c= D3768 ②+O3043 ①/ d=D926 ②+O423 ①/ e=D927 ②+D647 ①/ f=D927 ②+D928 ①/ g=O423 ②+O431 ①/ h=D930 ②+D3033 ①/ i=D926 ②+D927 ①

※ Add the circled numbers for the total number of strands per thread piece. Example: ②+①=3-strand thread

※ D = DMC, C = cosmo, O = Olympus

1st row characters back st. a
g g
Straight st.

2nd row characters back st. b
g h i g i

3rd row characters back st. c
i g g i g

4th row characters back st. d
g i g h

5th row characters back st. e
i g i g h

6th row characters back st. f
g i

70

Yacht Tarts with Embroidered Flags

See photo on page 11/Recipe for Yacht Tarts on page facing page 96

Materials (per flag)

White linen: 4" x 6" (10cm x 15cm)
Lightweight fusible interfacing: 2¾" x 5⅛" (7cm x 13cm)
Toothpick: 1

Finished dimensions (metric measurements are more
  precise)
3⅜" x 2⅛" (8.5cm x 5.5cm)

1. Trace design onto fabric and embroider

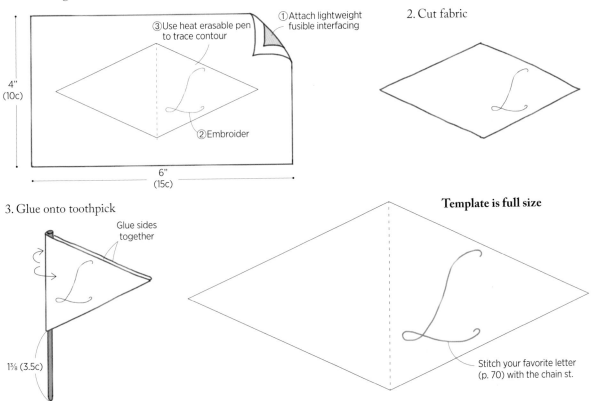

③Use heat erasable pen
to trace contour

①Attach lightweight
fusible interfacing

②Embroider

4"
(10c)

6"
(15c)

2. Cut fabric

3. Glue onto toothpick

Glue sides
together

1⅜ (3.5c)

Template is full size

Stitch your favorite letter
(p. 70) with the chain st.

Table Linens with European Motifs

See photos on pages 12, 13

Embroidery thread colors

※ The numbers within [ ] represent DMC corresponding color numbers.

DMC 647 (Silver Khaki) / 928 (Baby Sky Blue)

cosmo 366 [3782] (Ecru)

Olympus 421 [822] (Pearl Gray) / 430 [3024] (Silver Gray) / 431 [3023] (Soft Khaki)

Used for all D928②+D647①

Outline st.

Couching st.

Enlarge design by 125%

Used for all
O421②+O430①

Back st.

Outline st.

Used for all
C366②+O431①

Padded satin
stitch for all
Satin st.

Pincushions Made from Flea Market Finds

See photo on page 14

Embroidery thread colors

※ The numbers within [ ] represent DMC corresponding color numbers.

DMC 613 (Off-White) / 644 (Khaki White) / 822 (Milk White) / 926 (Dark Aqua) / 928 (Baby Sky Blue) / 930 (Dark Blue) / 3024 (Snow White) / 3768 (Iron Blue) / 3865 (White) / 3866 (Whitewash)

cosmo 151 [3024] (Cold White)

Olympus 316 [930] (Night Blue) / 354 [322] (Light Sky) / 430 [3024] (Silver Gray) / 3043 [3768] (Saxe Blue)

Color combination guide

a=O316 ①+O3043 ①/ b=O354 ②+D3768 ①/ c=D926 ②+D928 ①/ d=C151 ①+O430 ①/ e=D3768 ②+O354 ①/ f=D3768 ①+O354 ①/ g=D644 ①+D822 ①/ h=O354 ①+O3043 ①/ i=D3865 ①+D3866 ①/ j=O316 ①+O354 ①/ k=D822 ②+D613 ①/ L=D3024 ②+D3866 ①/ m=D3866 ②+D3024 ①

※ Add the circled numbers for the total number of strands per thread piece. Example: ②+①=3-strand thread, ①+①=2-strand thread

※ D = DMC, C = cosmo, O = Olympus

Design is full size

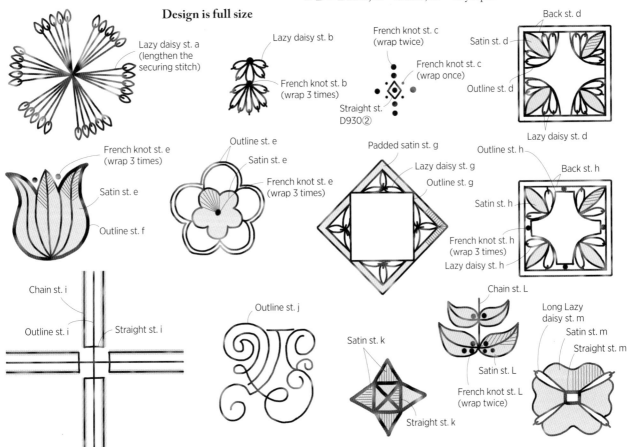

73

Coasters

See photo on page 15

Materials (per coaster)

Navy or white canvas: 8⅝" x 8⅝" (22cm x 22cm) 2 pieces
Leather: ⅜" x 1" (0.8cm x 5cm) 1 piece

Finished dimensions (metric measurements are more precise)

4¾" x 4¾" (12cm x 12cm)

Embroidery thread colors (same for all 3 coasters)

※ The numbers within [ ] represent DMC corresponding
color numbers.

DMC 613 (Off-White) / 646 (Khaki) / 712 (Warm White)
/ (Dark Aqua) / 3021 (Espresso) / 3750 (Midnight Blue) /
3768 (Iron Blue) / 3808 (Dark Blue Green) / 3842 (Blue)

cosmo 369 [3781] (Bronze)

Olympus 415 [3021] (Graphite) / 421 [822] (Pearl Gray)

Color combination guide (Design i)

a=D926 ②+D3768 ①/ b=D926 ②+O415 ②/ c=D3750
②+D3808 ①/ d= D3808 ②+D3750 ①+D3842 ①/ e=D646
①+O421 ①/ f=D613 ②+D712 ②

Color combination guide (Design ii)

a=D3808 ②+D3750 ①/ b=D646 ①+O421 ①/ c=C369
②+D3021 ①/ d= D3750 ②+D646 ①/ e=D712 ②+D3750 ①

Color combination guide (Design iii)

a=D712 ②+D613 ①/ b=D3808 ②+D3842 ①/ c=O421
②+D712 ①/ d= D646 ②+O415 ①/ e=D613 ②+D712 ②/
f=D3750 ②+D3808 ②/ g=D3750 ②+D3808 ①+D3842 ①/
h=D712 ②+O421 ②/ i=D926 ②+D3768 ①

※ Add the circled numbers for the total number of strands
per thread piece. Example: ②+①=3-strand thread,
①+①=2-strand thread

※ D = DMC, C = cosmo, O = Olympus

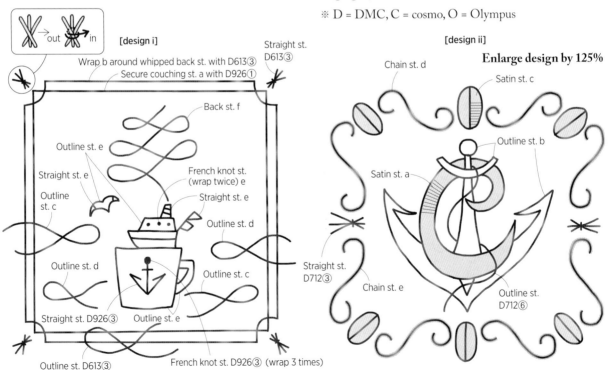

[design i]

out / in

Wrap b around whipped back st. with D613③
Secure couching st. a with D926①

Straight st. D613③

Back st. f

Outline st. e

Straight st. e

Outline st. c

French knot st. (wrap twice) e

Straight st. e

Outline st. d

Outline st. d

Outline st. c

Straight st. D712③

Straight st. D926③   Outline st. e

Outline st. D613③

French knot st. D926③ (wrap 3 times)

[design ii]

Enlarge design by 125%

Chain st. d

Satin st. c

Outline st. b

Satin st. a

Chain st. e

Outline st. D712⑥

1. Embroider on outer fabric

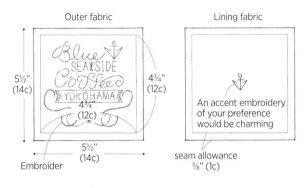

Outer fabric

Lining fabric

5½"
(14c)

4¾"
(12c)

4¾"
(12c)

5½"
(14c)

Embroider

An accent embroidery
of your preference
would be charming

seam allowance
⅜" (1c)

2. With right sides together, sew outer and lining fabrics

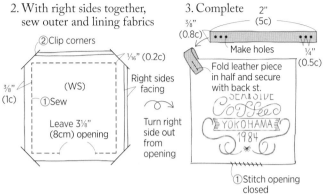

②Clip corners

1/16" (0.2c)

⅜"
(1c)

(WS)

①Sew

Right sides
facing

Leave 3⅛"
(8cm) opening

Turn right
side out
from
opening

3. Complete

2"
(5c)

⅜"
(0.8c)

Make holes

¼"
(0.5c)

Fold leather piece
in half and secure
with back st.

①Stitch opening
closed

Enlarge design by 125%

[design iii]

Outline st. a

Outline st. d

Straight st. d

Outline st. d

Back st. b
(Use straight st.
for straight line)

Straight st. a

Outline st. c

Wrap f around
whipped back st. e

Back st. i

Outline st. g

Fly st. i

Straight st. i

Back st. a

Back st. h

Straight st.
D712②

Wrap d around
straight st. d

out

in

Shell Pincushions

See photos on page 18, 19

Embroidery thread colors

※ The numbers within [ ] represent DMC corresponding color numbers.

DMC 159 (Hyacinth) / 613 (Off-White) / 646 (Khaki) / 647 (Silver Khaki) /
950 (Baby Pink) / 3024 (Snow White) / 3768 (Iron Blue) / 3865 (White) / 3866 (Whitewash)
cosmo 151 [3024] (Cold White)
Olympus 354 [322] (Light Sky) / 422 [648] (Olive Khaki) / 430 [3024] (Silver Gray) / 3043 [3768] (Saxe Blue)

Design is full size

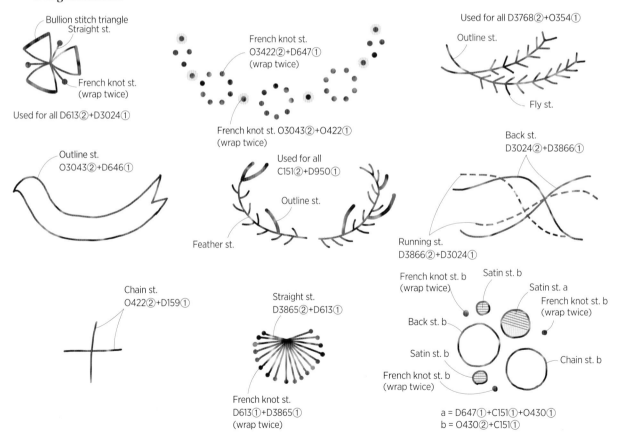

Bullion stitch triangle
Straight st.

French knot st.
(wrap twice)

Used for all D613②+D3024①

French knot st.
O3422②+D647①
(wrap twice)

French knot st. O3043②+O422①
(wrap twice)

Used for all D3768②+O354①

Outline st.

Fly st.

Outline st.
O3043②+D646①

Used for all
C151②+D950①

Outline st.

Feather st.

Back st.
D3024②+D3866①

Running st.
D3866②+D3024①

Chain st.
O422②+D159①

Straight st.
D3865②+D613①

French knot st.
D613①+D3865①
(wrap twice)

French knot st. b
(wrap twice)

Satin st. b

Satin st. a

French knot st. b
(wrap twice)

Back st. b

Satin st. b

Chain st. b

French knot st. b
(wrap twice)

a = D647①+C151①+O430①
b = O430②+C151①

Sea Urchin Shell Pincushions

See photo on page 21

Materials (per pincushion)

White linen: 6" x 6"(15cm s 15cm) 1 piece
Wool batting: as needed
Delica Beads (MIYUKI): as needed
Felt or leather: 1¼"(3.2cm) diameter, 1 piece

Finished dimensions (metric measurements
are more precise)

2⅛" (5.5cm) diameter x 1⅛" (3cm) high

Embroidery thread colors

※ The numbers within [ ] represent
DMC corresponding color numbers.

DMC 712 (Warm White) / 926 (Dark
Aqua) / 928 (Baby Sky Blue) / 3866
(Whitewash)

cosmo 151 [3024] (Cold White) / 366
[3782] (Ecru)

Olmpus 413 [646] (Gray) / 421 [822]
(Pearl Gray) / 431 [3023] (Soft Khaki)

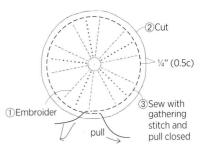

1. Except for the straight st.
embroider and cut the fabric

②Cut
¼" (0.5c)
①Embroider
③Sew with gathering stitch and pull closed
pull

2. Fill with wool batting and
embroider with straight st.

③Straight st.
②Adjust shape
①Insert wool batting

3. Glue felt (or leather)
on the bottom

Glue a round piece of felt or leather

diameter 1¼" (3.2c)

Design • Template is full size

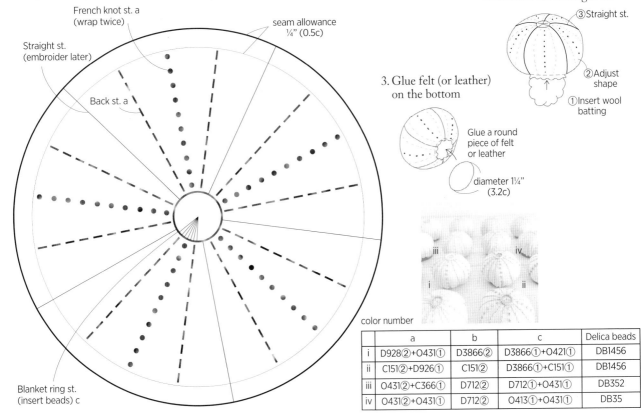

French knot st. a (wrap twice)

seam allowance ¼" (0.5c)

Straight st. (embroider later)

Back st. a

Blanket ring st. (insert beads) c

color number

	a	b	c	Delica beads
i	D928②+O431①	D3866②	D3866①+O421①	DB1456
ii	C151②+D926①	C151②	D3866①+C151①	DB1456
iii	O431②+C366①	D712②	D712①+O431①	DB352
iv	O431②+O431①	D712②	O413①+O431①	DB35

77

Sea Glass Sampler

See photo on page 22

Embroidery thread colors

※ The numbers within [ ] represent DMC corresponding color numbers.

DMC 613 (Off-White) / 928 (Baby Sky Blue) / 3024 (Snow White) / 3768 (Iron Blue) / 3799 (Charcoal Gray) / 3865 (White) / 3866 (Whitewash)

cosmo 151 [3024] (Cold White)

Olympus 415 [3021] (Graphite) / 421 [822] (Pearl Gray) / 430 [3024] (Silver Gray) / 431 [3023] (Soft Khaki) / 3043 [3768] (Saks Blue)

Color combination guide

a=D3866 ②+D3865 ①/ b=C151 ②+O430 ①/ c=D3024 ②+D928 ①/d=O430 ②+O421 ①/ e=C151 ②+D3865 ①/ f=D613 ②+D928 ①/ g=D3768 ②+O415 ①/ h=O415 ②+D3768 ①/ i=O431 ①+O3043 ①/ j=D3799 ①+O415 ①

※ Add the circled numbers for the total number of strands per thread piece. Example: ②+①=3-strand thread, ①+①=2-strand thread

※ D = DMC, C = cosmo, O = Olympus

Fill in the scroll with the embroidered, stamped or hand written text of your choice.

Enlarge design by 125%

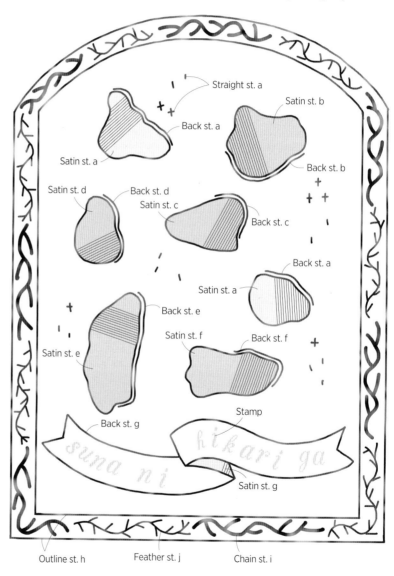

Framed Minerals

See photo on page 23

Embroidery thread colors

※ The numbers within [ ] represent DMC
   corresponding color numbers.

DMC 169 (Smoke Blue) / 413 (Blue Gray)
/ 645 (Olive) / 647 (Silver Khaki) / 926
(Dark Aqua) / 930 (Dark Blue) / 3024
(Snow White) / 3866 (Whitewash)

cosmo 151 [3024] (Cold White) / 890 [648]
(White Gray)

Olympus 423 [646] (Khaki Gray) / 431
[3023] (Soft Khaki)

Color combination guide

a=D169 ①+C151 ①+C890 ①/ b=D169
①+O423 ①+O431 ①/ c=D169 ①+D413
①+O423 ①/ d=C890 ①+O423 ①+O431
①/ e=D645 ①+D647 ①+D930 ①/ f=D169
① +D926 ①+O431 ①/ g=C151 ①+O431
①+D3866 ①/ h=D3866 ②+D3024 ①/
i=D645 ②+D926 ①

※ Add the circled numbers for the total
   number of strands per thread piece.
   Example: ②+①=3-strand thread,
   ①+①+①=3-strand thread

※ D = DMC, C = cosmo, O = Olympus

Design is full size

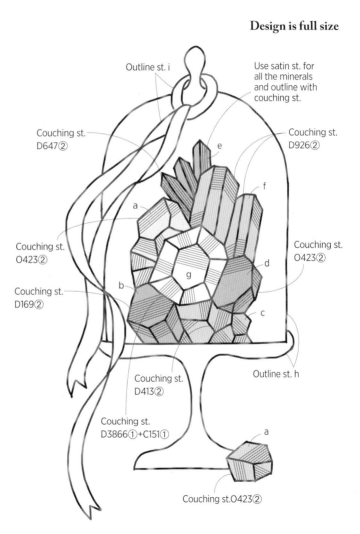

Outline st. i

Use satin st. for
all the minerals
and outline with
couching st.

Couching st.
D647②

Couching st.
D926②

e

f

a

Couching st.
O423②

Couching st.
O423②

b

g

d

Couching st.
D169②

c

Couching st.
D413②

Outline st. h

Couching st.
D3866①+C151①

a

Couching st.O423②

Embroidery thread colors

※ The numbers within [ ] represent DMC corresponding color numbers.

DMC 169 (Smoke Blue) / 535 (Steel Gray) / 610 (Hazelnut) / 613 (Off-White) / 648 (Pearl Gray) / 930 (Dark Blue) / 935 (Forest Green) / 3022 (Moss Green) / 3781 (Cinnamon) / Diamant 168 (Silver) / 5-strand•924 (Dark Navy) / 5-strand•3021 (Espresso)

cosmo 366 [3782] (Ecru) / 368 [611] (Dark Beige)

Olympus 354 [322] (Light Sky) / 413 [646] (Gray) / 3043 [3768] (Saxe Blue)

Color combination guide

a=D935 ②+O3043 ①/ b=D935 ②+D169 ①/ c=O3043 ②+D3022 ①/ d=D5 5-strand • 924 ①+D5 5-strand • 3021 ①/ e=O413 ②+C368 ①/ f=C366 ②+D613 ①+D648 ①/ g=D535 ②+D3781 ①/ h=D930 ②+O3043 ①+O354 ①/ i=D610 ②+D169 ①

※ Add the circled numbers for the total number of strands per thread piece. Example: ②+①=3-strand thread, ①+①=2-strand thread

※ D = DMC, C = cosmo, O = Olympus

Cotton Flower Pincushions
See photo on page 25

Materials (per pincushion)

White linen: 4¾" (12cm) diameter
Quilt batting: 2" x 6" (5cm x 15cm)
Suede: 4" x 4" (10cm x 10cm)
Mohair yarn (white): as needed

Wool batting as needed

Finished dimensions*

2" (5cm) diameter x 1⅛" (3cm) high

Embroidery thread colors

DMC 839 (Fallen Leaf)

Template ②
1 piece of suede

Design • Template is full size

Cotton Flower Pincushion

Template ①
5 pieces of quilt batting

Chain st. i

b

a

Fly st. (back st. tip only)

Lazy daisy st. d

a

Framed Winter Plants
See photo on page 24

Outline st.

c

Chain st. i

e

a

Outline st. g

Tie DMC Diamant 168③ into a ribbon

Lazy daisy st. Mohair yarn (White)
※ embroider extra straight st. at the core

French knot st. h (wrap twice)

Outline st. g

Outline st. e

a

b

Lazy daisy st. f

c

c

Lazy daizy st. for this design

Straight st. → → Straight st.

*Metric measurements are more precise.

Sea Voyage Bag I

See photo on page 26 / instructions on page 85

Embroidery thread colors

※ The numbers within [ ] represent DMC corresponding color numbers.

DMC 535 (Steel Gray) / 926 (Dark Aqua) / 3768 (Iron Blue)

Olympus 354 [322] (Light Sky)

Color combination guide

a=D926 ②+O354 ①/ b=D3768 ②+D535 ①

※ Add the circled numbers for the total number of strands per thread piece.
Example: ②+①=3-strand thread

※ D = DMC,
   O = Olympus

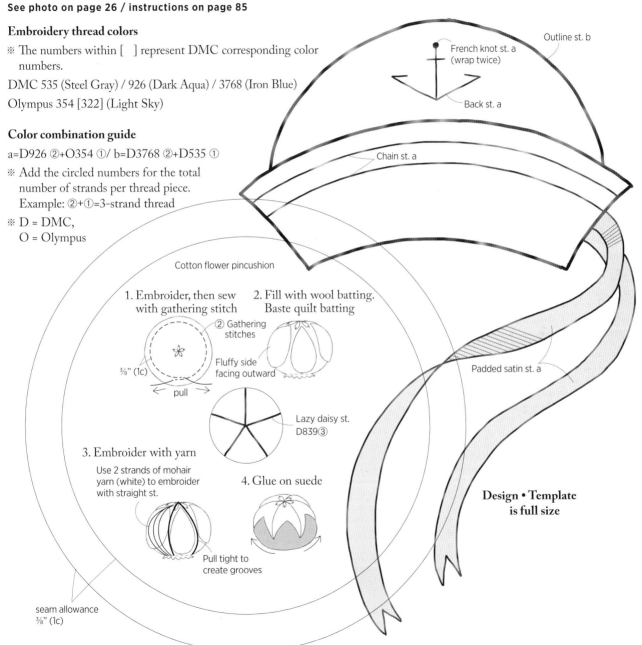

Outline st. b

French knot st. a
(wrap twice)

Back st. a

Chain st. a

Padded satin st. a

Cotton flower pincushion

1. Embroider, then sew with gathering stitch

② Gathering stitches

⅜" (1c)

pull

Fluffy side facing outward

2. Fill with wool batting. Baste quilt batting

Lazy daisy st. D839③

3. Embroider with yarn

Use 2 strands of mohair yarn (white) to embroider with straight st.

4. Glue on suede

Pull tight to create grooves

Design • Template is full size

seam allowance ⅜" (1c)

Sea Voyage Bag II

See photo on page 27 / instructions on page 85

Embroidery thread colors

※ The numbers within [   ] represent DMC
   corresponding color numbers.

DMC 613 (Off-White) / 3033 (Ivory)

Design is full size

Outline st. for all
D3033②+D613①

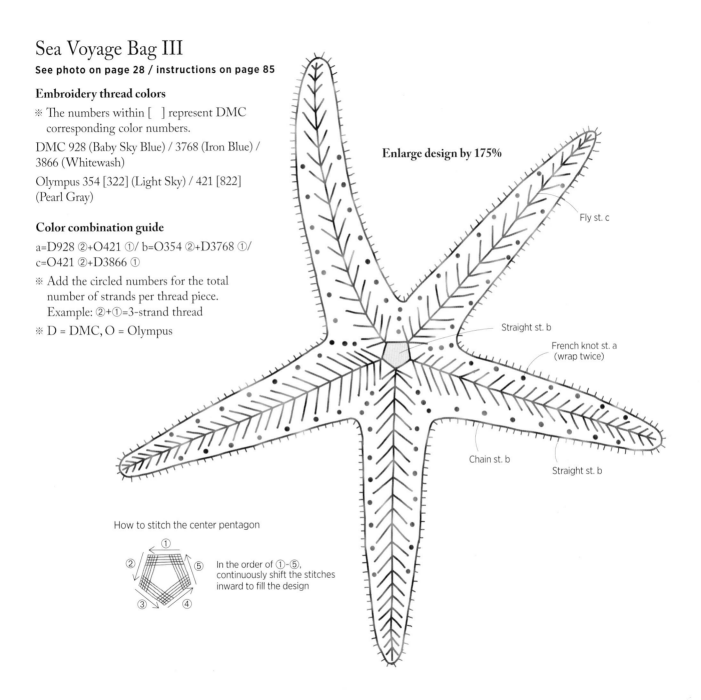

Sea Voyage Bag III

See photo on page 28 / instructions on page 85

Embroidery thread colors

※ The numbers within [ ] represent DMC
corresponding color numbers.

DMC 928 (Baby Sky Blue) / 3768 (Iron Blue) /
3866 (Whitewash)

Olympus 354 [322] (Light Sky) / 421 [822]
(Pearl Gray)

Color combination guide

a=D928 ②+O421 ①/ b=O354 ②+D3768 ①/
c=O421 ②+D3866 ①

※ Add the circled numbers for the total
number of strands per thread piece.
Example: ②+①=3-strand thread

※ D = DMC, O = Olympus

Enlarge design by 175%

Fly st. c

Straight st. b

French knot st. a
(wrap twice)

Chain st. b

Straight st. b

How to stitch the center pentagon

In the order of ①-⑤,
continuously shift the stitches
inward to fill the design

Sea Voyage Bag IV

See photo on page 29 / instructions on page 85

Design is full size

Embroidery thread colors

※ The numbers within [ ] represent
   DMC corresponding color numbers.

DMC 3768 (Iron Blue) / 3866
   (Whitewash)
cosmo 151 [3024] (Cold White)
Olympus 3043 [3768] (Saxe Blue)

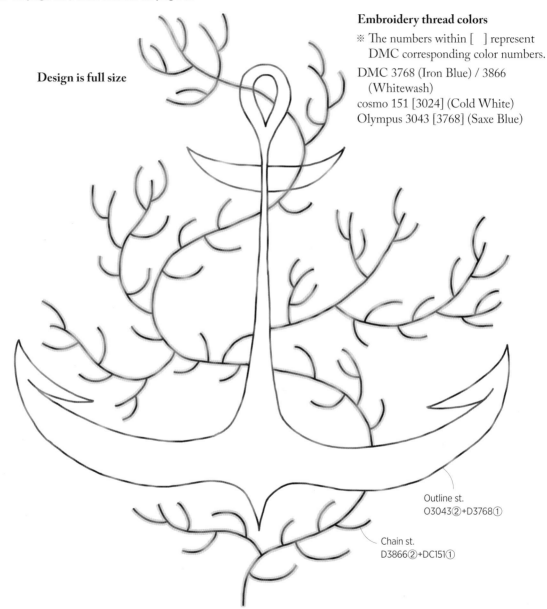

Outline st.
O3043②+D3768①

Chain st.
D3866②+DC151①

Sea Voyage Bag I ~ IV

See photos on pages 26 ~ 29

Materials (per bag)

I   White cotton: 7¾ x 25⅝" (45cm x 65cm)
II Blue linen: 29½" x 15¾" (75cm x 40cm)
III White canvas: 43¼" x 19¾" (110cm x 50cm)
IV Aqua linen: 29½" x 15¾" (75cm x 40cm)

Finished dimensions (metric measurements are more precise)

I   10⅝" x 9" (27cm x 23cm) (Not including handles)
II/IV 10" x 9" (25cm x 23cm) (Not including handles)
III 15" x 13⅜" (38cm x 34cm) (Not including handles)

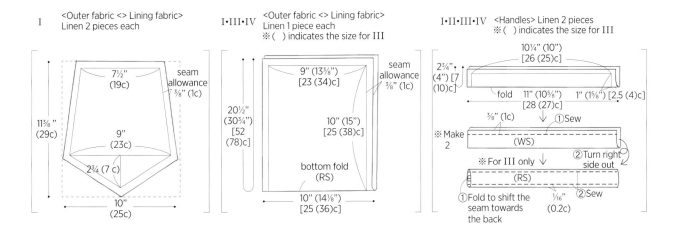

1. Embroider on outer fabric (front side)

2. Make outer bag and bag lining

3. Attach handles to outer bag and bag lining

4. Turn right side out and stitch opening closed

5. Stitch handles

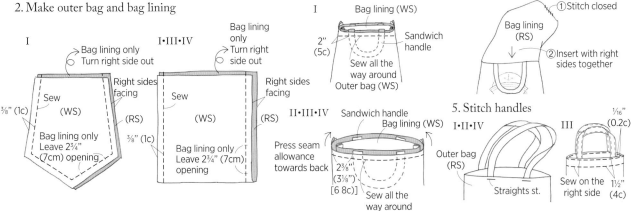

Large Shawl with Acorn Designs

See photos on pages 30, 31

Materials (per coaster)

Blue linen: 43¼" x 43¼" (110cm x 110cm)
Gray linen: 43¼" x 43¼" (110cm x 110cm)
Wool yarn: as needed

Finished dimensions (metric measurements
are more precise)

39⅜" x 39⅜" (100cm x 100cm)

Embroidery thread colors

※ The numbers within [ ] represent DMC corresponding color numbers.

※ Extra fine wool could be substituted for Appleton

Appleton 151 (Ice White) / 153 (Horizon Blue) / 926 (Navy Blue) / 972 (Grayish Brown) / 973 (Chocolate) / 987 (White Smoke)

DMC 648 (Pearl Gray) / 926 (Dark Aqua) / 928 (Baby Sky Blue) / 3033 (Ivory) / 3768 (Iron Blue) / 3790 (Mocha) / 3866 (Whitewash)

cosmo 366 [3782] (Ecru) / 367 [612] (Café Au Lait) / 369 [3781] (Bronze)

Olympus 421 [822] (Pearl Gray) / 431 [3024] (Soft Khaki) / 3043 [3768z] (Saks Blue)

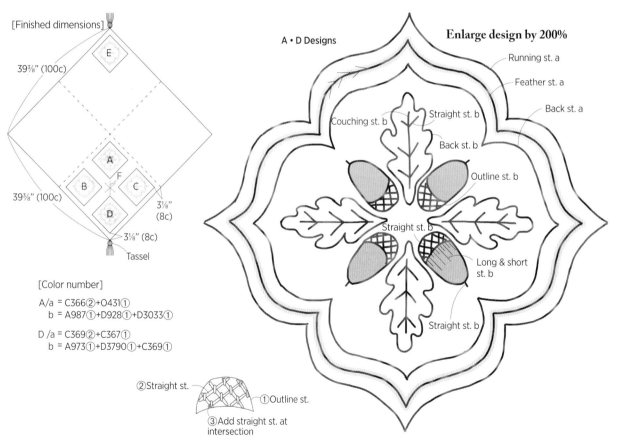

[Finished dimensions]

39⅜" (100c)

39⅜" (100c)

E

A

F

B   C

D

3⅛" (8c)

3⅛" (8c)

Tassel

[Color number]

A/a = C366②+O431①
   b = A987①+D928①+D3033①

D /a = C369②+C367①
   b = A973①+D3790①+C369①

A • D Designs

Enlarge design by 200%

Running st. a

Feather st. a

Back st. a

Couching st. b

Straight st. b

Back st. b

Outline st. b

Straight st. b

Long & short st. b

Straight st. b

②Straight st.

①Outline st.

③Add straight st. at intersection

86

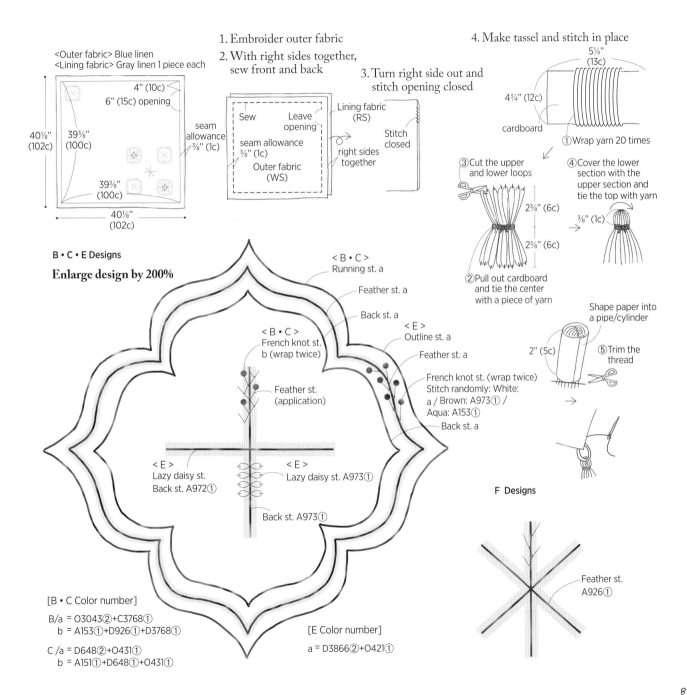

<Outer fabric> Blue linen
<Lining fabric> Gray linen 1 piece each

1. Embroider outer fabric
2. With right sides together, sew front and back
3. Turn right side out and stitch opening closed
4. Make tassel and stitch in place

4" (10c)
6" (15c) opening

40⅛" (102c)
39⅜" (100c)
39⅜" (100c)
40⅛" (102c)

seam allowance ⅜" (1c)

Sew
Leave opening

Lining fabric (RS)

seam allowance ⅜" (1c)

Stitch closed

Outer fabric (WS)

right sides together

5⅛" (13c)
4¾" (12c)
cardboard

①Wrap yarn 20 times

③Cut the upper and lower loops

2⅜" (6c)
2⅜" (6c)

②Pull out cardboard and tie the center with a piece of yarn

④Cover the lower section with the upper section and tie the top with yarn

⅜" (1c)

Shape paper into a pipe/cylinder

2" (5c)

⑤Trim the thread

B • C • E Designs

Enlarge design by 200%

< B • C >
Running st. a

Feather st. a

Back st. a

< B • C >
French knot st. b (wrap twice)

< E >
Outline st. a

Feather st. a

French knot st. (wrap twice)
Stitch randomly: White: a / Brown: A973① / Aqua: A153①

Back st. a

Feather st. (application)

< E >
Lazy daisy st.
Back st. A972①

< E >
Lazy daisy st. A973①

Back st. A973①

F Designs

Feather st. A926①

[B • C Color number]

B/a = O3043②+C3768①
  b = A153①+D926①+D3768①

C /a = D648②+O431①
  b = A151①+D648①+O431①

[E Color number]

a = D3866②+O421①

Ship Pouches

See photos on pages 32

Materials (per pouch)

Canvas (Blue • Aqua • Off-White): 12" x
  23¾" (30cm x 60cm)
Cotton: 12" x 23¾" (30cm x 60 cm)
Heavyweight fusible interfacing: ⅞" (2cm)
  diameter, 2 pieces
⅜" (0.8cm) diameter magnetic snap: 1 set
¼" (0.6cm)- wide ribbon: 2" (5cm)

Finished dimensions (metric measurements
  are more precise)

8" x 4" (20cm x 10cm) (boxed corner)
  x 4" (10cm) high

Embroidery thread colors (same for all 3 pouches)

※ The numbers within [ ] represent DMC corresponding color numbers.

DMC 648 (Pearl Gray) / 822 (Milk White) / 3768 (Iron Blue) / 3799
(Charcoal Gray) / 3866 (Whitewash)

cosmo 151 [3024] (Cold White)

Olympus 421 [822] (Pearl Gray)

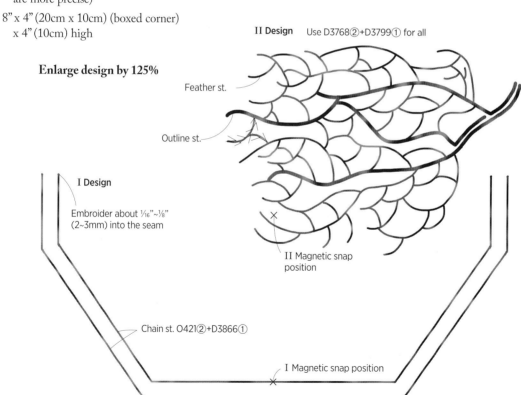

Enlarge design by 125%

II Design   Use D3768②+D3799① for all

Feather st.

Outline st.

I Design

Embroider about ¹⁄₁₆"~⅛"
(2~3mm) into the seam

II Magnetic snap
position

Chain st. O421②+D3866①

I Magnetic snap position

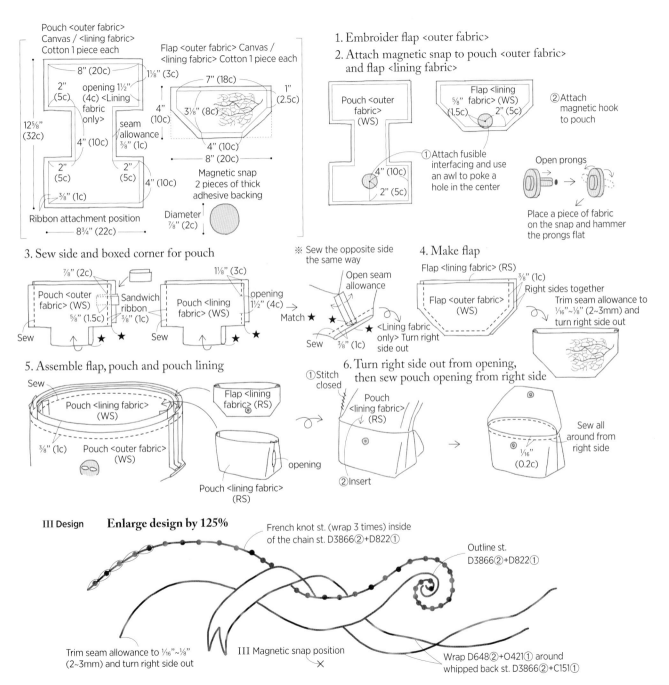

Pouch <outer fabric>
Canvas / <lining fabric>
Cotton 1 piece each

8" (20c)
1⅛" (3c)
2" (5c)
opening 1½" (4c) <Lining fabric only>
12⅝" (32c)
seam allowance ⅜" (1c)
4" (10c)
2" (5c)
2" (5c)
4" (10c)
⅜" (1c)
Ribbon attachment position
8¾" (22c)

Flap <outer fabric> Canvas /
<lining fabric> Cotton 1 piece each

7" (18c)
1" (2.5c)
4" (10c)
3⅛" (8c)
4" (10c)
8" (20c)
Magnetic snap
2 pieces of thick adhesive backing
Diameter ⅞" (2c)

1. Embroider flap <outer fabric>
2. Attach magnetic snap to pouch <outer fabric> and flap <lining fabric>

Pouch <outer fabric> (WS)

Flap <lining fabric> (WS)
⅝" (1.5c)
2" (5c)

②Attach magnetic hook to pouch

4" (10c)
2" (5c)

①Attach fusible interfacing and use an awl to poke a hole in the center

Open prongs

Place a piece of fabric on the snap and hammer the prongs flat

3. Sew side and boxed corner for pouch

⅞" (2c)
Pouch <outer fabric> (WS)
Sandwich ribbon
⅝" (1.5c)
⅜" (1c)
Sew
★ ★

1⅛" (3c)
opening 1½" (4c) →
Pouch <lining fabric> (WS)
Sew
★ ★
Match ★

※ Sew the opposite side the same way

Open seam allowance

<Lining fabric only> Turn right side out
Sew ⅜" (1c)

4. Make flap

Flap <lining fabric> (RS)
⅜" (1c)
Flap <outer fabric> (WS)
Right sides together
Trim seam allowance to ¹⁄₁₆"~⅛" (2~3mm) and turn right side out

5. Assemble flap, pouch and pouch lining

Sew
Pouch <lining fabric> (WS)
Flap <lining fabric> (RS)
⅜" (1c)
Pouch <outer fabric> (WS)
opening
Pouch <lining fabric> (RS)

6. Turn right side out from opening, then sew pouch opening from right side

①Stitch closed
Pouch <lining fabric> (RS)
②Insert

Sew all around from right side
¹⁄₁₆" (0.2c)

III Design   **Enlarge design by 125%**

French knot st. (wrap 3 times) inside of the chain st. D3866②+D822①

Outline st. D3866②+D822①

Trim seam allowance to ¹⁄₁₆"~⅛" (2~3mm) and turn right side out

III Magnetic snap position
✕

Wrap D648②+O421① around whipped back st. D3866②+C151①

Straw Tote Cover

See photo on page 34

Materials

White canvas: 27½" x 39⅜" (70cm x 100cm)
Blue cotton: 27½" x 39⅜" (70cm x 100cm)
Wool yarn: as needed

Finished dimensions (metric measurements are more precise)

17⅜" x 20¾" (44cm x 53cm) (laid flat)

Embroidery thread colors (same for all 3 pouches)

※ The numbers within [ ] represent DMC corresponding color numbers.

DMC 613 (Off-White) / 648 (Pearl Gray) / 712 (Warm White) / 92 (Dark Aqua) / 927 (Aqua) / 3768 (Iron Blue) / 3866 (Whitewash)

cosmo 151 [3024] (Cold White) / 366 [3782] (Ecru) / 5-strand • 600 [310] (Black)

Olympus 421 [822] (Pearl Gray) / 431 [3023] (Soft Khaki)

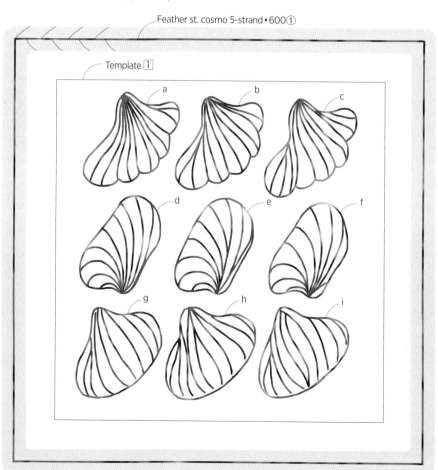

Feather st. cosmo 5-strand • 600①

Template 1

Design • Template is full size

Use outline st. for all shells [color number]

a = C366①+O431①
b = D3866①+O421①
c = D926①+O431①
d = D926①+C151①
e = D648①+O421①
f = D3866①+C151①
g = D613①+D712①
h = D3927①+O431①
i = D926①+D3768①

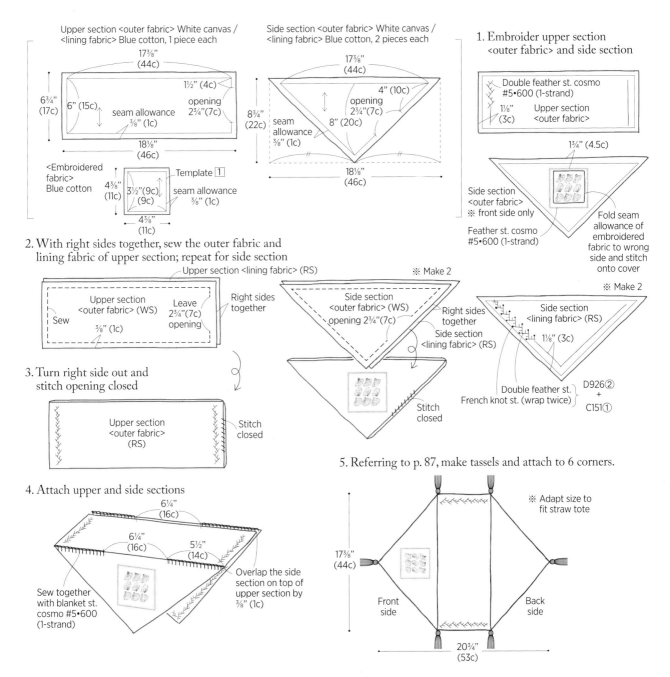

Upper section <outer fabric> White canvas /
<lining fabric> Blue cotton, 1 piece each

17⅜" (44c)

1½" (4c)

6¾" (17c)

6" (15c)

opening
2¾"(7c)

seam allowance
⅜" (1c)

18⅛" (46c)

<Embroidered fabric>
Blue cotton

Template ①

4⅜" (11c)

3½"(9c) (9c)

seam allowance
⅜" (1c)

4⅜" (11c)

Side section <outer fabric> White canvas /
<lining fabric> Blue cotton, 2 pieces each

17⅜" (44c)

4" (10c)

opening
2¾"(7c)

8¾" (22c)

seam allowance
⅜" (1c)

8" (20c)

18⅛" (46c)

1. Embroider upper section
<outer fabric> and side section

Double feather st. cosmo
#5•600 (1-strand)

1⅛" (3c)

Upper section
<outer fabric>

1¾" (4.5c)

Side section <outer fabric>
※ front side only

Feather st. cosmo
#5•600 (1-strand)

Fold seam allowance of embroidered fabric to wrong side and stitch onto cover

2. With right sides together, sew the outer fabric and
lining fabric of upper section; repeat for side section

Upper section <lining fabric> (RS)

Upper section
<outer fabric> (WS)

Leave 2¾"(7c) opening

Sew

⅜" (1c)

Right sides together

※ Make 2

Side section
<outer fabric> (WS)
opening 2¾"(7c)

Right sides together

Side section
<lining fabric> (RS)

Stitch closed

※ Make 2

Side section
<lining fabric> (RS)

1⅛" (3c)

Double feather st.
French knot st. (wrap twice)

D926②
+
C151①

3. Turn right side out and
stitch opening closed

Upper section
<outer fabric>
(RS)

Stitch closed

4. Attach upper and side sections

6¼" (16c)

6¼" (16c)

5½" (14c)

Sew together
with blanket st.
cosmo #5•600
(1-strand)

Overlap the side section on top of upper section by ⅜" (1c)

5. Referring to p. 87, make tassels and attach to 6 corners.

※ Adapt size to
fit straw tote

17⅜" (44c)

Front side

Back side

20¾" (53c)

Embroidered Drawstring Bags

See photos on page 35

Materials (per bag/determine preferred bag size)

※ Materials listed is for a bag with finished dimensions 10¼" x 8" (26cm x 20cm)

White linen: 23⅝" x 12" (60cm x 30cm)
Drawstring: 39⅜" (100cm)
All inch measurements are approximate.

Embroidery thread colors

※ The numbers within [ ] represent DMC corresponding color numbers.

DMC 535 (Steel Gray) / 712 (Warm White) / 928 (Baby Sky Blue) / 3768 (Iron Blue) / 3866 (Whitewash)

cosmo 151 [3024] (Cold White) / 366 [3782] (Ecru)

Olympus 354 [322] (Light Sky) / 423 [646] (Khaki Gray) / 431 [3023] (Soft Khaki)

Design is full size

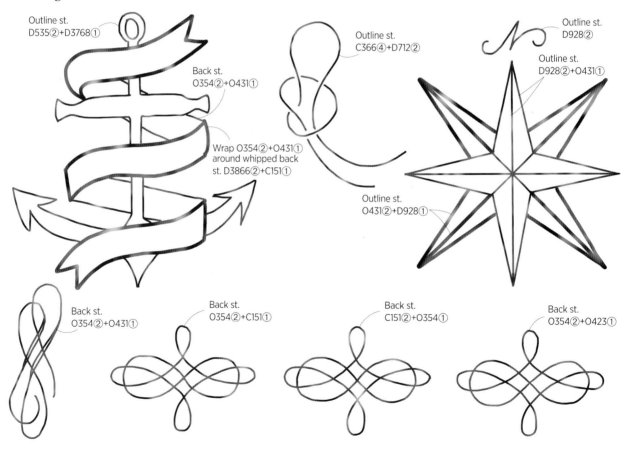

Outline st. D535②+D3768①

Back st. O354②+O431①

Wrap O354②+O431① around whipped back st. D3866②+C151①

Outline st. C366④+D712②

Outline st. D928②

Outline st. D928②+O431①

Outline st. O431②+D928①

Back st. O354②+O431①

Back st. O354②+C151①

Back st. C151②+O354①

Back st. O354②+O423①

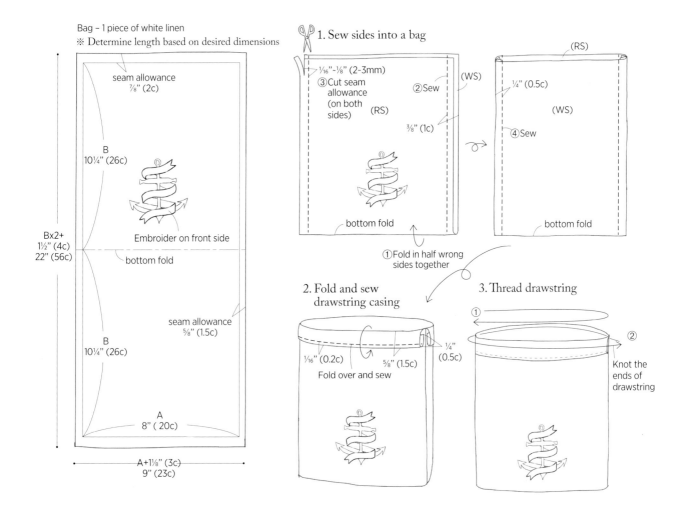

Bag – 1 piece of white linen
※ Determine length based on desired dimensions

seam allowance
⅞" (2c)

B
10¼" (26c)

Embroider on front side

bottom fold

Bx2+
1½" (4c)
22" (56c)

seam allowance
⅝" (1.5c)

B
10¼" (26c)

A
8" (20c)

A+1⅛" (3c)
9" (23c)

1. Sew sides into a bag

1/16"~⅛" (2-3mm)
③Cut seam
allowance
(on both
sides)   (RS)

②Sew

(WS)

⅜" (1c)

(RS)

¼" (0.5c)

(WS)

④Sew

bottom fold

bottom fold

①Fold in half wrong
sides together

2. Fold and sew
drawstring casing

1/16" (0.2c)

Fold over and sew

⅝" (1.5c)

¼"
(0.5c)

3. Thread drawstring

①

②

Knot the
ends of
drawstring

Keychain Charms

See photos on page 36

Materials (per keychain charm)

Gray linen: 6" x 6" (15cm x 15cm)
Suede: 4" x 2" (10cm x 5cm)
Eyepin: 1
Jump ring • Key ring: 1 each
Decorative ribbon • Embroidery
  thread: as needed

Finished dimensions (embroidered section)*

2¼"–2¾" x ⅞"–1¼"(5.7~7cm ×
  2~3.2cm)

Embroidery thread colors

※ The numbers within [ ] represent DMC corresponding color numbers.

DMC 535 (Steel Gray) / 926 (Dark Aqua) / 927 (Aqua) / 928 (Baby Sky Blue) /
3768 (Iron Blue) / 3866 (Whitewash) / Diamant 168 (Silver) / Diamant 3821 (Gold)
/ Diamant 3852 (Antique Gold)

cosmo 151 [3024] (Cold White) / Silk thread no. 22 (Champagne Gold)

Olympus 354 [322] (Light Sky) / 421 [822](Pearl Gray) / 431 [3023] (Soft Khaki)

Color combination guide

a=D927 ②+O431 ①/ b=D3866 ②+C151 ①/ c=O354 ②+D926 ①/
d=D3866 ②+C151 ①/ e=D535 ②+D3768 ①/ f=D928 ②+O421 ①

※ Add the circled numbers for the total number of strands per thread piece.
    Example: ②+①=3-strand thread

※ D = DMC, C = cosmo, O = Olympus

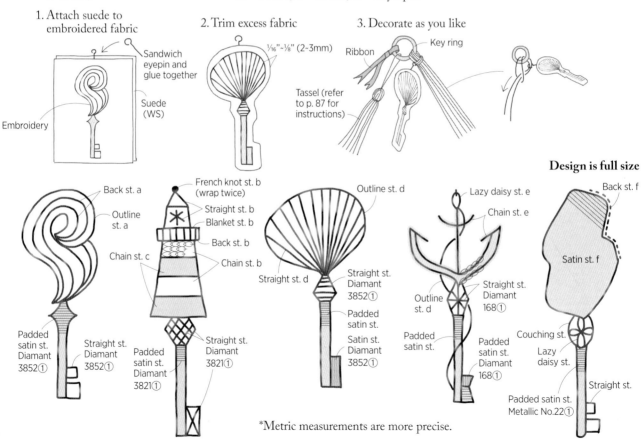

1. Attach suede to embroidered fabric

Embroidery

Sandwich eyepin and glue together

Suede (WS)

2. Trim excess fabric

1/16"~1/8" (2~3mm)

3. Decorate as you like

Ribbon

Key ring

Tassel (refer to p. 87 for instructions)

Design is full size

Back st. a
Outline st. a
Chain st. c
Padded satin st. Diamant 3852①
Straight st. Diamant 3852①

French knot st. b (wrap twice)
Straight st. b
Blanket st. b
Back st. b
Chain st. b
Padded satin st. Diamant 3821①
Straight st. Diamant 3821①

Outline st. d
Straight st. Diamant 3852①
Padded satin st.
Satin st. Diamant 3852①
Straight st. d

Lazy daisy st. e
Chain st. e
Outline st. d
Straight st. Diamant 168①
Padded satin st.
Padded satin st. Diamant 168①

Back st. f
Satin st. f
Couching st.
Lazy daisy st.
Straight st.
Padded satin st. Metallic No.22①

*Metric measurements are more precise.

Embroidered Bracelet

See photo on page 37

Materials

Aqua linen: 8" x 12" (20cm x 30cm)
⅞" (2cm)- wide Ribbon crimp end: 2
Jump ring: 2
Key ring: 1
Lobster clasp: 1
¼" (0.6cm)- wide ribbon: as needed

Finished dimensions (metric measurements are more precise)

1⅛" x 6¼" (3cm x 16cm) (Not including ribbon).

Embroidery thread colors

※ The numbers within [ ] represent DMC corresponding color numbers.

DMC 413 (Blue Gray) / 645 (Olive) / 3033 (Ivory)

Color combination guide

a=D645 ①+D413 ①/ b=D3033 ①+C151 ①

※ Add the circled numbers for the total number of strands per thread piece. Example: ①+①=2-strand thread

※ D = DMC, C = cosmo

Design is full size

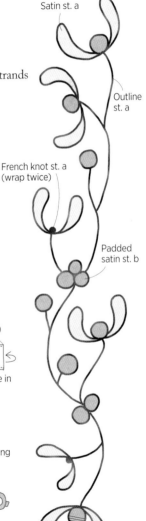

Satin st. a

Outline st. a

French knot st. a (wrap twice)

Padded satin st. b

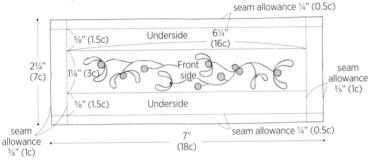

seam allowance ¼" (0.5c)

Underside 6¼" (16c)

⅝" (1.5c)

2¾" (7c)

1⅛" (3c)   Front side

seam allowance ⅜" (1c)

⅝" (1.5c)   Underside

seam allowance ⅜" (1c)

7" (18c)

seam allowance ¼" (0.5c)

1. Sew with right sides together

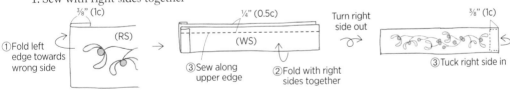

⅜" (1c)

(RS)

①Fold left edge towards wrong side

¼" (0.5c)

(WS)

③Sew along upper edge

②Fold with right sides together

Turn right side out

⅜" (1c)

③Tuck right side in

2. Attach metal parts

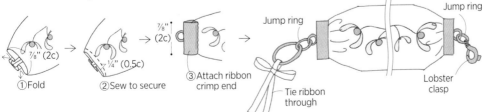

⅞" (2c)

¼" (0.5c)

①Fold

②Sew to secure

⅞" (2c)

③Attach ribbon crimp end

Jump ring

Tie ribbon through

Jump ring

Lobster clasp

Books to Span the East and West

Our core mission at Tuttle Publishing is to create books which bring people together one page at a time. Tuttle was founded in 1832 in the small New England town of Rutland, Vermont (USA). Our fundamental values remain as strong today as they were then—to publish best-in-class books informing the English-speaking world about the countries and peoples of Asia. The world is a smaller place today and Asia's economic, cultural and political influence has expanded, yet the need for meaningful dialogue and information about this diverse region has never been greater. Since 1948, Tuttle has been a leader in publishing books on the cultures, arts, cuisines, languages and literatures of Asia. Our authors and photographers have won many awards and Tuttle has published thousands of titles on subjects ranging from martial arts to paper crafts. We welcome you to explore the wealth of information available on Asia at **www.tuttlepublishing.com**.

Published by Tuttle Publishing, an imprint of Periplus Editions (HK) Ltd.

www.tuttlepublishing.com

AO TO SHIRO NO SHISHU (NV70528)
Copyright © Kozue Yazawa/ NIHON-VOGUE-SHA 2019
All rights reserved
English translation rights arranged with NIHON VOGUE, Corp. through Japan UNI Agency, Inc., Tokyo
Photographers: Yukari Shirai, Kozue Yazawa

English Translation © 2021 Periplus Editions (HK) Ltd.
Translated from Japanese by Sanae Ishida

Original Japanese edition
Book Design Mina Hanawa (ME & MIRACO)
Cover photography Yukari Shirai
Project photography Kozue Yazawa
Illustrations/Designs Yuriho Koike
Editing Mio Nishizu

Distributed by

North America, Latin America & Europe
Tuttle Publishing
364 Innovation Drive, North Clarendon,
VT 05759-9436 U.S.A.
Tel: 1 (802) 773-8930
Fax: 1 (802) 773-6993
info@tuttlepublishing.com
www.tuttlepublishing.com

Asia Pacific
Berkeley Books Pte. Ltd.
3 Kallang Sector #04-01, Singapore 349278
Tel: (65) 6741 2178
Fax: (65) 6741 2179
inquiries@periplus.com.sg
www.tuttlepublishing.com

23 22 21 20   10 9 8 7 6 5 4 3 2 1
Printed in Malaysia   2010VP

ISBN 978-0-8048-5399-6

Yacht Tarts (page 11)

[Makes sixteen 2" x 4" (5cm x 10cm) boats]

Note: This recipe was created using gram measurements, and using those if possible will yield more precise results.

You will need

Your favorite baking tools
Boat-shaped tart molds

Dough

Cake/pastry flour, about 1⅛ cups (150g)
1 tsp water
Egg yolk 1 (20g)
Granulated sugar 1¼ tsps (5g)
Pinch of salt
Unsalted butter, about ½ cup (100g)

Cream

Unsalted butter about ⅓ cup (70g)
Granulated sugar about ⅓ cup (70g)
Eggs 1-2 (70g)
Almond four or almond meal about ⅝ cup (70g)
2 tsps of a liqueur such as Cointreau or Rum (optional)

Toppings

Sliced almonds
Shredded coconut
Dry pine needles

1. To make the dough, first chill the flour in the refrigerator.
2. Add the water to the yolk (to obtain a total of about 25g liquid). Mix in the sugar, then the salt, and chill in the fridge.
3. The butter should be soft enough break up. Cut the butter into the flour with a pastry blender or spatula to form a grainy texture.
4. Add in the liquid mixture (be careful not to knead).
5. Chill in the fridge for at least an hour, or up to overnight.
6. Roll out the dough to about ⅛" (3mm) thick and form into boats. Pierce with a fork.
7. Preheat the oven to 400° (200°C).
8. Next, make the cream. Warm the butter to room temperature. Whisk the sugar into the butter.
9. Lightly beat the eggs (1-3 turns with the whisk). Mix into the butter with your whisk.
10. Add the almond flour/meal and blend in with the spatula. (To make the coconut flavoring, mix in with the almond flour/meal before adding). Add your liqueur or other flavoring. Mix in with a rubber spatula.
11. Mix the cream with a flavor of your choice and add toppings such as (1) A mixture of lemon extract (about 1¼ tbs [20 ml]) + grated lemon zest. Top with sliced almonds. (2) Coconut flavoring (replace half of the almond flour/meal with fine macaroon coconut). Top with shredded coconut. (C) 16 dry pine needles + 2 tsps (10 ml) lemon extract + 1 tsp (5 ml) ginger extract. Top with dry pine needles.
12. Fill four boats with the cream and add the topping of your choice. Top the lemon extract portion with sliced almonds, the coconut flavoring portion with shredded coconut, and the last portion with dry pine needles.
13. Place in preheated over for 8 minutes, reduce temperature to 355° (180°C) and bake for another 5 minutes.
14. Remove from the mold when cool, add the embroidered flags, and sail!